POWERPRO SERIES

MECHANIC'S GUIDE TO
PRECISION
MEASURING TOOLS

Forbes Aird

MBI Publishing Company

First published in 1999 by MBI Publishing Company, 729 Prospect Avenue, PO Box 1, Osceola, WI 54020-0001 USA

MBI Publishing Company books are also available at discounts in bulk quantity for industrial or sales-promotional use. For details write to Special Sales Manager at Motorbooks International Wholesalers & Distributors, 729 Prospect Avenue, Osceola, WI 54020-0001 USA.

Library of Congress Cataloging-in-Publication Data
Aird, Forbes.
   Mechanic's guide to precision measuring tools/Forbes Aird.
      p. c.—(PowerPro)
   Includes index.
   ISBN 0-7603-0545-5 (pbk.: alk. paper)
   1. Measuring instruments. 2. Gauges. I. Title. II. Series: powerpro series.
TJ313.A35   1999
681.2—dc21   99-17761

On the front cover: Ultimate performance begins with precision measuring! From alignment gauges to Vernier micrometers, all of the tools you may ever require to measure a gap, span, angle, radius, pitch, force, pressure, or flow with the resolution and accuracy of a professional are meticulously described and demonstrated in the Mechanic's Guide to Precision Measuring Tools. *David Gooley*

On the back cover: (Top, left): Leak-down testers, sometimes called differential pressure testers, give a good picture of the state of an engine's valves and rings. The difference in reading between the two gauges indicates how fast air is leaking past those seals. This engine is mighty tight, with no visible difference between the two readings. *Karl Fredrickson photo, courtesy Open Wheel magazine* (Right): Dial indicators are comparative instruments. While the distance from the crank centerline to the block deck surface (the "deck height") may be of interest, of arguably greater importance is its uniformity from end to end and side to side. A fixed-length gauge bar allows a dial indicator to gauge this dimension. *Powerhouse Products* (Below): Small hole gauges based on the "split-ball" principle are used to measure holes below the lower limit of telescoping gauges. Turning the knurled knob at the end pulls on a tapered wedge that expands the ball. Once the user has confirmed by "feel" that the setting is correct, the span across the two halves of the ball is measured with a micrometer. *L.S. Starrett Company*

Edited by John Adams-Graf

Designed by Pat Linder

Printed in the United States of America

CONTENTS

Acknowledgments 5

Introduction 7

CHAPTER 1
The Idea of Precision 9
Why Precision Measurement
Accuracy versus Precision
Reference Standards
Analog versus Digital Measurements
Some Notes on the Metric System

CHAPTER 2
Measuring a Span (Part 1) 17
The Machinist's Rule
The Combination Square
Outside Calipers
Slide Calipers
Using Slide Calipers
Fixed Gauges
Height Gauges

CHAPTER 3
Measuring a Span (Part 2) 28
The Micrometer Caliper
Reading a Micrometer
The Vernier Micrometer
Reading a Vernier Micrometer
The Use of Micrometers
The Dial Indicator
Use of the Dial Indicator
Dial Test Indicators
The Gauge Blocks

CHAPTER 4
Measuring a Gap 47
Inside Calipers
Slide Calipers
Taper Gauges
Telescoping Gauges
Small-Hole Gauges
Thickness ("Feeler") Gauges
Plastigage™
Inside Micrometers
Bore Micrometers
Dial Bore Gauges
Depth Gauges

CHAPTER 5
Measuring Angles, Radii, and Pitches 62
Angular Measurements
Straightedges, Parallels, and the
    Machinist's Square
Levels
The Angle Finder
Bevel Protractors
Timing Wheels/Degree Wheels
The Sine Bar
Precision Angle Blocks
Fixed Gauges
Gauging Threads

CHAPTER 6
Measuring Weights, Forces, and Pressures 78
Mechanical Weight Scales (Balances)
Electronic Weigh Scales
Force Gauges
Torque Wrenches
Using a Torque Wrench
Measuring Pressures and Vacuum
The "U"-Tube Manometer
Other Pressure Gauges
Leak-Down Testers

CHAPTER 7
Miscellaneous Measuring Tools 102
Volt/Ohm/Ammeters
Using a Multimeter
Measuring Temperature
Liquid-in-Glass Thermometers
Dial Thermometers
Pyrometers
Thermocouples
Noncontact Pyrometers
Tachometers
Timing Lights
Measuring Volumes
Alignment Gauges and Tools

APPENDIX
Conversion Factors for Pressure 125
Index 127

ACKNOWLEDGMENTS

This, my ninth book, my sixth for Motorbooks, has been by far the easiest and most pleasant to work on of all to date. This is due in no small part to the wonderful helpfulness and cooperation of the many people and firms I had occasion to pester for information.

My thanks to Jim McCann of Torque Tools Canada for valuable leads; to Dave Friedel of Starrett-Weber for fascinating insight into the issue of absolute reference standards; to Scott Robinson, John Richardson, Paul Nault, and Dexter Carlson of the L.S. Starrett Company; to Susan Hurley of The Do-All Corporation; to Robert Palumbo of Brown & Sharpe; to Aaron Friedman and Michael Goldberg of Eastern Technology Corporation for explanations about the subtleties surrounding the use of leak-down testers; to Ken Walsh of Interweigh Systems and Mark Morris at Mettler-Toledo for detail on the delicate art of weighing things; to racer-turned-robot designer Gord Green for insight into the workings of tachometers; to Jim Dunham at Percy's High Performance; to Marty Block at Argo Manufacturing; to Ray Reinerton of Sturtevant-Richmond and Tom Becker of Snap-On Tools for helpful information about torque wrenches; to Mark Brown at Intercomp for an explanation of the workings of digital caster/camber gauges; finally, to Paul Rieker of Kinsler Fuel Injection. If I have missed anyone, my thanks anyway, and apologies for imperfect note-taking.

Many of these same companies also provided photos and illustrations for the book. They are credited as they appear; my thanks to all of them. In addition, I am again indebted to Doug Gore, Robin Hartford, and Karl Fredrickson of *Open Wheel* and *Stock Car Racing* magazines for kindly providing photographs that appeared in those publications, and to their editor, Dick Berggren, for permitting me to use them here.

INTRODUCTION

"When you can measure what you are talking about, and express it in numbers, you know something about it; but when you cannot express it in numbers, your knowledge is of a meagre and unsatisfactory kind . . ."

William Thomson, Lord Kelvin, said that sometime between 1891 and 1894. It is surely no coincidence that the introduction of the micrometer occurred at almost exactly the same moment in history.

If mechanical technology has not quite become perfected in the century since, at the very least it is now a thoroughly mature branch of applied science. Consider the products of that technology we now take for granted—the modern passenger car, reliable as a stove; jet travel; mass-produced consumer goods, with interchangeable parts, by the countless millions . . . None of this would have been possible without precision measuring tools.

A mere handful of years before Lord Kelvin's pronouncement, almost none of these tools existed; the few that did were the jealously guarded possessions of a handful of toolmakers, the most revered craftsmen of the day. Now they are available (and, equally important, *affordable*) to most anyone. This book is an attempt to explain the design and working principles of some of those tools, and to describe their correct use.

The selection of which tools to include in this book has been made with that issue of affordability in mind. Accordingly, we have made no mention of air gauging, nor laser-equipped alignment rigs, nor advanced electronic devices that need a roomful of flashing lights and bells and whistles for their use. Of course, the professional who needs to perform precision measurements on a daily basis can justify the purchase of seriously expensive tools as a business investment, but most of the measuring instruments and tools dealt with here are well within the reach of the serious amateur.

Before launching into the subject, it seems appropriate to point out at the beginning that the act of measuring something inevitably changes the thing being measured. Now, sometimes this effcct is so small as to be immeasurable. For example, when we set a rule down beside something and read the object's size off the rule, we need light to see the result. Theoretically, the photons of light bombarding the object change its size. And sometimes the effect is large enough to be measured, yet so small as to be irrelevant for all practical purposes. Thus, the act of closing a micrometer onto a 1/8-inch steel rod squashes the rod by about two-millionths of an inch, so it measures smaller than it really is. Sometimes, though, we have to take pains to avoid serious inaccuracies from this cause. If you stick a thermometer in a cup of hot coffee to measure its temperature, the cool thermometer will soak up some of the heat, so the measured temperature of the coffee will be quite noticeably lower than it was before we tried to measure it.

While every measurement is an approximation, we hope to show how, by understanding the inherent limitations of precision measuring tools and by using them in a way that minimizes user errors, the degree of uncertainty in measurements can be brought within tolerable limits. Then your knowledge will be of an abundant and satisfactory kind.

C
O
N
T
E
N
T
S

Why Precision
Measurement 9

Accuracy versus Precision . 11

Reference Standards 12

Analog versus Digital
Measurements 15

Some Notes on the Metric
System 16

CHAPTER ONE

THE IDEA OF PRECISION

Why Precision Measurement?

Contrary to popular wisdom, you can, in fact, fit a square peg in a round hole . . . provided you have a large enough hammer. Where you may run into trouble is fitting a *round* peg in a round hole . . . if the peg is much larger than the hole. If you have a peg that is too large for the hole you want to fit it in, you have a few choices. If you have a sizable collection of holes and pegs, you can find another hole or another peg that does fit. Alternatively, you can whittle the peg down somewhat; or you can ream the hole out, to make it larger.

In the world of engineering and mechanics, the mixing-and-matching of parts to find a set that can live happily with each other is called "selective fitting," while the peg-shaving and hole-auguring are simply called "fitting." Some old-timers still remember the tedious filing and grinding and lapping and scraping that used to be part of the arsenal of skills of the machinist/mechanic; Englishmen of a certain age still call such people "fitters." Indeed, when your grandpa was a lad, obtaining a good "fit" between mating parts of a machine was very often achieved in that way. Bearings were scraped to conform to the crank journals, pistons were filed (yes, filed) to establish a serviceable clearance in the cylinder bores, and shim-stock and machinist's blue (an oily dye that rubs off

to reveal high spots) were found in every mechanic's toolbox.

You don't see a lot of piston filing going on these days, and if the bearings don't fit, you bark at the parts counter and send 'em back. Likewise, the use of selective fit seems part of an era of steam and whirling brass and 6-foot flywheels with spokes.

The difference between then and now is a matter of being able to control the dimensions of manufactured goods within very tight limits, and of being able to measure those dimensions with high accuracy. Thus, the people who grind crankshafts and those who make engine bearings (and likewise those who machine pistons and bore cylinders) can control the sizes of those parts, and can express the pertinent measurements, with sufficient precision and accuracy that a suitable fit between corresponding parts can be achieved just on the basis of their listed sizes. It is this ability to maintain dimensional control that makes possible the concept of interchangeable parts, and interchangeable parts are essential for the mass production of complex mechanisms.

The idea of interchangeable parts dates back a long time. In 1785, Thomas Jefferson wrote from Paris that, "An improvement is made here in the construction of muskets, which may be of interest to Congress . . . It consists of the making of every part of them so exactly alike, that what belongs to any one may be used for every other musket in the magazine." Fifteen years later, Eli Whitney achieved a degree of interchangeable manufacture in his armament business.

The benefits of doing things this way were convincingly demonstrated in 1908, when Henry Leland shipped three of his Model A Cadillacs to Britain, to compete for the Dewar Trophy. There, under the skeptical eyes of officers of the Royal Automobile Club, the three cars were taken for a drive, then dismantled entirely, and their parts mixed up haphazardly. From the random heap of shafts, gears, bolts, and innumerable other bits, three cars were reassembled and run vigorously on the road once more, without trouble. The trophy was duly awarded, and Leland departed, triumphant.

Obviously, it is only mass production that makes it possible to manufacture automobiles in large quantities, and to sell them at a price per pound that compares favorably with steak. So, precise and accurate measurement is a basic requirement for making interchangeable parts, and interchangeable parts are essential for mass production, which is what allows us to have cars to work on in the first place.

Paradoxically, from the point of view of one individual working on one specific project, the interchangeability of parts, while certainly a convenience, may not be absolutely vital—he can always resort to "fitting." But fitting, too, requires measurement, and the closer the fit, the more accurate the measurement must be—those old mechanics' toolboxes equipped with shim-stock and machinist's blue also invariably contained micrometers.

There is more. Most automotive enthusiasts are concerned about performance, but no matter how you define performance, improving it means, in general, getting more from less. Whether it be judged in terms of acceleration, top speed, cornering ability, or fuel economy, increasing performance usually involves working parts harder—subjecting them to larger loads, requiring them to turn at higher speeds, operating them at higher temperatures. And as the loads, speeds, and temperatures go up, the need for accurately sized parts, and so the necessity of accurately measuring those parts, increases.

An example: The main and connecting rod bearing clearance specified for most passenger car engines typically runs somewhere in the neighborhood of 0.0015 inch to 0.0035 inch—the crank journal is smaller than the inside diameter of the bearing shell by that amount, and the difference between the least permissible clearance and the greatest (called the *tolerance*) is 0.002 inch. Now, some amount of clearance is needed simply for the shaft to be able to turn within the bearing and for an oil film of some minimum size to fit between the two; also, a little allowance has to be made for the expansion of parts with heat. Anything more than that minimum necessary amount, however, means more oil leakage out of the ends of the bearings, which drops oil pressure. Also, excessive clearance means the bearings are subject to a pounding every time the slack gets taken up. Both effects threaten the life of the bearings. As a result, engines for race use are usually built with "tighter" clearances—0.0020 to 0.0025 inch, for example. (Note

that the bearing does not necessarily fit the crank any "tighter," it is simply that the tolerance is narrowed.) To achieve those more rigorous specifications, the measurements have to be correspondingly finer and more exact.

In the same way, the combustion chambers of a production engine might vary in volume by as much as 5 percent, so while one cylinder is operating at a compression ratio (C.R.) of near 10:1 and be on the brink of detonating, its neighbor might be comparatively loafing along at little more than 9:5, wasting potential power. To get all the cylinders working equally hard, we want all the cylinders to be operating at the highest practical C.R. That requires that we be able to measure the volume of each combustion chamber with considerable accuracy.

In the matter of cornering and handling, the various dimensions that affect alignment likewise become increasingly critical as the demands increase. While production passenger cars might specify camber with a tolerance of ± 1/2 a degree or more, the independent suspension system on road race cars can be sensitive to camber changes of less than a tenth of a degree. Similarly, oval track racers can detect a change in lap times resulting from an increase or decrease of tire pressure of just 1 or 2 psi, or a change in "stagger" (the difference in diameter between the two rear tires) of some small fraction of an inch.

The list is endless. Indeed, almost every effort to improve a vehicle's performance requires the ability to measure some physical quantity to a higher level of precision and accuracy than economical mass production demands or permits. These, then, are the reasons precision measurement is important.

Accuracy versus Precision

As I sit here at my keyboard, a digital clock in my office informs me that the time right . . . NOW, is 4:04:32 P.M. Well, that is a statement of considerable *precision*. It implies that 32 seconds, but not yet 33, have passed since it was 4:04, although it might be getting very, very close to 4:04:33. So, the maximum possible imprecision is 1 second. Now, there are 24 hours in a day, 60 minutes in each hour, and 60 seconds in each minute, thus there are 86,400 seconds in a day, so my digital clock seems to claim a maximum possible imprecision of 1 part in 86,400. In other words, a precision of better than 99.9988 percent. Considering that the thing was free in the first place, I should be mighty pleased. I am not . . . because I know perfectly well that the stupid thing is at least a couple of minutes slow! *Precise* it may be, *accurate* it is not.

On the other hand, I also have in my office an old wind-up clock, the sort that ticks. Given my funky old eyesight and the fact that the clock is a good three strides away, all I can say about the time it is telling me is that it is "somewhere around 5 after 4." Now this is a very much less precise statement than the first. Indeed, it is at least 120 times less precise, since I don't have a hope in hell of reading the old ticker with any better accuracy than plus-or-minus 1 minute—120 seconds, in total. On the other hand, it turns out that the information I am able to gain from it is more accurate.

The first point to be made, then, is that precision and accuracy are not the same thing. Precision can be defined as the quality of being sharply or clearly determined. A precision measuring instrument is one that expresses the property it is measuring as some very small fraction of a reference unit, whether that unit is an inch, a day, a pound, or a gallon. A closely related idea is *resolution*, which is the smallest graduation into which an instrument is divided. You can measure more precisely with a rule marked in sixteenths of an inch than with one marked only in quarters, because the first one has a higher resolution. Neither precision nor resolution guarantees accuracy, however, as the following true story shows.

A guy I know needed a workshop. Because he lives in an isolated, largely inaccessible spot, he contracted the construction of the building as a prefabrication, to be delivered in half a dozen pieces. Meanwhile, he poured his own concrete footings. When the shed arrived, there was a misfit of several inches between the prefab building and the concrete foundation. After much yelling and swearing between owner and contractor, they discovered that their tape measures (both with a resolution of 1/16 inch, but one a respected brand name, the other a no-name cheapie) differed by more than 2 inches in 20 feet! . . . which emphasizes the importance of *accuracy*: the degree to which an indicated value conforms to an accepted standard value.

The precision and accuracy of a measurement certainly depend on the quality and calibration of the tool being used for the measuring but also depend on the individual using that tool or instrument. Ask three different machinists or mechanics to measure the same object with the same micrometer and you will very likely get three different answers (though they are all likely to be within two or three ten-thousandths of each other).

Indeed, even if one person measures the same thing three times, you are still likely to get variations. One of the acid tests of a useful measurement is the degree to which it is repeatable.

While some authorities suggest that a measuring tool accurate to 0.01 inch precision or less can only offer a "coarse" measurement, and one accurate to 0.001 inch or better is a "precision" tool, precision is really a matter of degree; there is no fixed benchmark that determines whether or not a measurement is a "precise" one.

To some extent, it is a matter of the absolute size of the thing being measured. Measuring the wheelbase of a car with a precision of ± 0.10 inch (about 1 part per 1,000) would probably satisfy even the fussiest engineer concerned with calculations of, say, wheel loads during various maneuvers. Conversely, even 0.010 inch precision would be absurdly inadequate if the object of interest was, say, the tip of a metering rod from a Rochester carburetor, because these rods are only around 0.030–0.050 inch in diameter! To achieve 1 part per 1,000 precision here would require measuring to at least "half-a-tenth" accuracy (a thousandth of an inch is often abbreviated to "thou"; likewise, a ten-thousandth may be abbreviated to just "tenth," provided the context makes it clear that this is not a single tenth of an inch).

I suggest that, for our purposes, a length measurement accurate to 1 part in 1,000 is the least acceptable to qualify as "precision," while accuracy to 1 part in 10,000 is the highest we are likely to be able to achieve. So, when it comes to measuring lengths in the usual range of those that require a high level of precision in general shop work—say, from a few "thou" up to

6 inches—if you can get readings precise to 0.0005 inch, get your measurements to repeat within 0.0002–0.0003 inch, and can confirm that your measuring tool is accurate within ± 0.0001 inch, then you can take confidence that you are achieving an admirable level of accuracy and precision.

Reference Standards

Leland's ability to assemble three cars from randomly selected parts came more than a century after Eli Whitney first achieved the goal of interchangeable parts, yet the practice was still limited to one class of products, within one factory. Even Henry Ford, the father of mass production, was obliged in the early days to have his most skilled craftsmen build pilot models, using a great deal of hand fitting. The pilot models were then disassembled and their thousands of parts used as "master-pieces" (yep, that's where the expression comes from) for the calibration of production gauges. In a sense, dimensions were not expressed as "so many inches and so many thousandths," but rather as "exactly the same as this one here." As a result of this, manufacturing could not be carried on at any great distance from the parts that served as the reference dimensions.

This way of doing things had unarguable benefits over the previous methods of hand fitting (or selective fitting) virtually every part produced. But while the inconvenience of the "master-piece" method of calibration could be endured, within one factory, the whole procedure was obviously wasteful and inefficient. It is one thing to repeatedly make parts with uniform dimensions, it is another thing altogether to express those dimensions in a way that allows someone else, somewhere else, to make matching parts. And the difference is a universal standard of length.

Even though instruments were available in the mid-1800s that could measure to one-thousandth of an inch, the lack of a reference standard meant that Leland's party trick and Ford's production line represented surprisingly little progress beyond Whitney's pioneering efforts. And virtually no advance was made in this state of affairs until the 1920s.

It was World War I that forced a fundamental change. Individual factories could not produce, efficiently and economically, all of the separate parts that go to make up a tank, an artillery piece, or a battleship; the need to subcontract became vital. But to make this possible, a universal standard of length had to be established—everyone's tape measures had to have inches of the same length. Over the course of the next few years, the National Bureau of Standards took on the colossal job of calibrating and checking all master gauges used in the manufacture of munitions. Of course, that raises the question of what they were checked against.

The earliest reference lengths were based on the size of body parts—an inch was the width of a thumb, a foot the length of the part of your body that keeps your socks on, a yard the distance from the tip of a nose to the end of an outstretched hand, and so on. The problem with all this stuff, of course, is *whose* thumb? *Whose* foot? *Whose* nose? Perhaps the earliest attempt at establishing a permanent reference length was in 1558, after which date the yard was defined as the length of a bronze bar—"the Queen's yard"—kept as a standard by the King's Exchequer.

Little had changed by the time the National Bureau of Standards set about its formidable task during World War I. The reference unit of length was the Imperial yard, defined as the distance between two fine marks scratched on a metal bar. (That bar, presented to the United States in 1856, was in fact a duplicate, as exact a copy of the British original as could be achieved by comparing the placement of the scribe marks, using a microscope.) Between then and the U.S. involvement in the war, the practical problems of ensuring that workshop measurements corresponded to that standard—and could be traced back to it—was greatly eased by the invention of the gauge block.

A gauge block is simply a slab of metal, usually rectangular, having two finely ground and highly polished opposite faces, spaced some designated distance apart; on one of the other sides it bears an engraved figure indicating that dimension, plus a mark identifying the maker. Thus, a "1-inch" gauge block is the means by which "1 inch" is given physical form and made usable either as a direct unit of measurement or as a standard for calibrating an instrument that measures length.

To be useful as a calibration standard, however, the actual distance between the two working surfaces must be known and specified with a level of accuracy that is almost unimaginable. We are not talking here about "close enough for rock-'n-roll," or "within a couple of thou." No, we are talking about accuracy, in the case of laboratory master grade gauge blocks, of *one-millionth* of an inch. One-millionth! It is enough to make your hair stand on end. What is a millionth of an inch? Pluck out one of those hairs and divide it,

The Importance of Having a Good Figure: Significant Digits

When dealing with whole numbers and decimal fractions, scientists, engineers, and math teachers pay close attention to something called "significant digits." If you are going to be making use of precision measuring tools, you would do well to understand this concept. It bears on the fact that every measurement is an approximation, and that the way you express the result of a measurement (or a calculation) indicates the degree of certainty you are claiming . . . the limit of your precision, if you like.

Suppose two people measure the bore of an engine cylinder. The first uses a steel rule graduated in hundredths of an inch and announces the dimension to be 3.99 inches; the second uses an inside micrometer graduated in thousandths and declares the bore to measure 3.987 inches. Assuming that each has been as careful as possible, then each is arguably "correct," to a degree of precision appropriate to the tool he is using, but each has uncertainty about what lies beyond the last decimal place. It is conventionally accepted that, whatever the actual value of the uncertainty, it cannot be less than 5 in the next decimal place. Thus, the first individual is saying, in effect, that the dimension lies somewhere between 3.985 and 3.994, but he cannot be sure just where in that range the "true" answer lies, so he "rounds" his answer to two decimal places. The other is able to pin down the value more closely (to three decimal places), but his result is still approximate; he is, in reality, claiming that the "true" value is between 3.9865 and 3.9874 although, again, he cannot say just where. So, you do not lay claim to greater precision than the limits of the tool you are using, and you do not read more precision into someone's measurement than they express. Thus, for example,

it would be mistaken to assume, based on the rule measurement, that the bore measures 3.9900 inches.

So far, so good. But suppose we are using the more precise bore measurement to calculate the volume (displacement) of the cylinder (and let us suppose that we know the stroke to be 3.000 inches). The formula for computing the volume of a cylinder is:

$$\text{volume} = \text{bore}^2 \times 0.7854 \times \text{stroke}$$
$$= 3.9872 \times 0.7854 \times 3.000$$

The first place we might run into a problem is in "squaring" the value for the bore (that is, multiplying the number by itself). Note that we are multiplying together two numbers, each with three decimal places. If you do this long-hand, or use a calculator having enough digits in its display, the answer you will get is 15.896169. But we are now implying six-decimal accuracy based on a measurement with only three figures after the decimal point!

Things get even sillier if we continue the calculation in this way. After multiplying by 0.7854, we get a result with 10 decimal places!

The solution is to carry through to the end of the calculation, then to look back to determine the factor that has the fewest significant figures. Recognizing that the final answer cannot be any more precise than the least precise number involved in the calculation, you round the answer to that many places.

To do the rounding, you have to look at the next digit after the cutoff point. If it is 5 or more, you "round up"; if 4 or less, you "round down." Thus, 3.14159 rounded to four places becomes 3.1416; rounded to three places, it is 3.142; and to two places, it is 3.14. Working that way, the volume of our cylinder is 37.455 cubic inches.

---

widthwise, 3,000 times.

The credit for the first gauge blocks is attributed variously to two Swedes: Hjalmar Ellstrom and C.E. Johansson, around the turn of the century. (Some machinists still refer to gauge blocks as "Johansson blocks" or "Jo blocks." "Jo-Block" is now a registered trademark.) The first gauge blocks produced in the

United States were made in 1918 by Major William Hoke, then head of the Gage [sic] Division of the United States Bureau of Standards.

It is reasonable to ask how it can be known for certain that the two working surfaces of a gauge block are, in fact, exactly 1 inch apart, give or take one-millionth of an inch. In Johansson's and Ell-

strom's and Hoke's day, it was still a matter of comparing the length of a chunk of metal to that of a reference piece—another chunk of metal—kept in a bureau of standards. All industrialized nations had some such national depository.

Today, the "universal inch" is defined to be exactly 25.4 millimeters. A millimeter, in turn, is exactly one-thousandth of a meter. And a meter is defined, not as the distance between a pair of scribe marks on a metal bar, but rather as the distance light travels in a vacuum in some incomprehensibly tiny fraction of a second, as measured by an atomic clock.

While the speed of light does not vary with temperature, nor humidity, nor the effects of gravity, nor even with one's location in the universe, nevertheless it appears, ultimately, that there really is no *absolute* reference for length. To explain, the speed of light, on which all this apparent precision hinges, was initially established by measuring the time taken for light to travel from a source, to a mirror, and back again. The trouble here arises in measuring the distance to the mirror, which can only be done using some sort of unit of length that, by the above definition, itself depends on the speed of light! When you get down deep enough, the whole argument seems to run around in circles.

In practical terms, we need not concern ourselves too much about this. Provided that everyone agrees what an inch is, it doesn't really matter if it is, "in fact," an inch and three-millionths . . . or an inch and three-quarters, for that matter, just as long as all our inches are the same length (give or take a millionth). Again, in practical terms, if we have a gauge block that came with a document certifying it to be some specific dimension, then we can use that gauge block to check and correct the accuracy of the micrometer we might use to measure a crankshaft journal with confidence that the bearings made by someone on the other side of town (or the other side of the country, or the other side of the world) will fit. Always provided that they cali-

brated their instruments against a gauge block of equal accuracy.

It is also reasonable to ask if this level of precision is really necessary, at least for the purposes of the sort of mechanical work most readers of this book are likely to be involved with. We have made mention of crankshaft and bearing diameters, which are invariably expressed as a number precise to within one-thousandth of an inch, or sometimes to within half of a thousandth. Even carb jets and metering rods are only expressed to, at most, 10 times that level of precision. There are few, if any, dimensions in any part of an automobile that need to be held any more accurate than that. Why, then, should we be discussing the issue of measurements 100 times more precise?

The answer lies partly in just exactly what it is we mean in terms of *precision* when we say something measures 0.002 inch, or 0.0020 inch, which we deal with in the sidebar on significant digits found below. Partly, too, it has to do with the *accuracy* with which we are able to measure such a dimension. It is generally accepted that the accuracy of a measuring instrument has to be at least 10 times greater than the degree of precision specified for the thing being measured. (In fact, this 10-to-1 ratio is pretty much a number pulled out of a hat. By using modern statistical methods, it is possible to prove that the calibrating device need be only about 4 times as accurate as the thing being calibrated. Still, when working with decimal fractions, the only way to get to the "next decimal place" is to use the 10-to-1 criterion.) So, if you want to measure accurate to, say, one-thousandth, then the instrument you measure with has to be accurate to at least

one ten-thousandth.

One ten-thousandth, however, is still 100 times more "vague" than one-millionth. But if we are to be confident in the reading offered by a micrometer, for example, we have to calibrate that micrometer against a reference—typically a gauge block—that is 10 times more accurate than the micrometer claims to be. Thus, the minimum level of accuracy and precision of that gauge block has to be in the order of a hundred-thousandth (that is, ten-millionths) of an inch. Now, if a set of micrometers is directly checked against a gauge block, there has to be some physical contact between the instrument and the block. Do that a few hundred times, and some imperceptible amount of material (an amount one three-thousandth the thickness of a human hair, perhaps?) will get rubbed off the block, and its accuracy will deteriorate.

To check the gauge block, we need even more accurate gauge blocks, which is the justification for laboratory master grade blocks of one-millionth accuracy. (To retain their accuracy, such masters are used only to calibrate working grade blocks.) Outside of laboratories such as the National Institute for Science and Technology (NIST), which are dedicated to confirming and refining national standards, one-millionth of an inch is as fine as we can get.

It might seem, based on the above discussion, that is plenty good enough for any purpose having to do with machinery. Astonishing as it may seem, there are, in fact, some fairly common situations where an even higher level of accuracy would be advantageous. If, for example, you buy two or more supposedly identical tapered roller bearings, complete with outer races, don't ever mix up the races. Here, as in every other case where there is a need to be any more precise than the current limits of economical mass production and the technology of measurement permit, we are stuck with (you may have guessed it!) selective fitting . . . each bearing and race set is a matched pair, sorted on that basis.

Analog versus Digital Measurements

Of the two clocks in my office, the first has a display (or "read-out") that consists of illuminated numbers, the other a dial and pointers. They are, respectively, digital and analog devices. A great many of the precision measuring tools discussed in the remainder of this book are offered in both analog and digital versions, so it seems worth spending a little time considering the respective benefits and drawbacks of the two types. (Incidentally, the digital ones are usually electronic, but there are also digital mechanical instruments, in which the read-out consists of engraved or photo-etched numbers that appear sequentially in a window.)

The first appearance of digital displays (at least, *electronic* digital displays) is within the memory of anyone now old enough to have trouble with their teeth. Perhaps their greatest advantage is that they express whatever it is they have to say in simple, unambiguous terms—if you can count up to 10, you can read a digital display without error. Indeed, digital measurement really amounts to counting; the display announces the whole number of steps, each of a certain size, between two fixed end-points.

Analog displays, on the other hand, take a bit more learning. For instance, children can generally read and report a numerical display quite a while before they can tell the time from a traditional clock. And some analog read-outs, such as a Vernier scale, demand even more from the viewer. Without sufficient experience and practice, or in dim light, or on a bad day, it is possible to make a reading that is wildly off.

The clear-cut message from a digital display greatly reduces the chance of such a misreading. One of the prices paid for this is that it also excludes reading "between the lines." If, for example, we use a rule marked in quarter-inch divisions to measure some dimension, and the value appears to fall exactly midway between 6 1/4 and 6 1/2 inches, then we can reasonably assume that the value is close to 6 3/8 inches. If we performed the same measurement using a digital device offering the same resolution (there are none; this example is just to make a point), it would insist that the measured value was *either* 6 1/4 *or* 6 1/2 inches. This sort of estimation between markings is generally frowned on; if a measurement winds up part way between divisions, then you really should either accept the limits of the tool you are working with and accept the reading of the closest mark, or use a more precise instrument. Still, when absolutely forced to do so by lack of equipment, it is possible to extend the limits of an analog measuring tool's precision in this way.

The inner workings of electronic digital measuring tools take various forms. Without going too deeply into this, let us just say that the working principle behind most affordable electronic digital instruments is one of "counting steps." The precision of the read-out, then, depends on the size of the steps that the instrument counts;

the smaller each step, the higher the potential precision. At the same time, the smallest step that can be meaningful has to be related to the accuracy of the instrument as a whole. (Generally, each of these "electronic" instruments is, in reality, a mechanical device with a step counter piggy-backed onto it.)

Another price to be paid for the convenience of a digital display is . . . um, the price to be paid. Digital electronic instruments are invariably more expensive than a comparable mechanical device. In the case of slide calipers from one well-known manufacturer, for example, the premium for the electronic version compared to its conventional dial-equipped counterpart is about 25 percent; in other cases, the price penalty can sometimes be 100 percent or more.

As to "ruggedness," it may be that a simple mechanical device is inherently more robust, and so less easily damaged, than one housing the electronics necessary for a digital display. Still, it would be misleading to pursue this argument any further; precision measuring tools are not monkey wrenches, and they should never be dropped or otherwise handled roughly. (I could tell you another true story, about a micrometer being used as an ignition wrench . . .)

Then there is the old issue about "what are you going to do when the batteries run flat?" Okay, so you keep some spares around, but there is bound to come a day when you are working with someone else's tools, and they do things "the old way." Even if you decide to have only electronic measuring tools in your own kit, there is still much to be said for learning how to read instruments "the old way," if only to avoid embarrassment. It also helps in the development of a keen sense of touch, which can be almost as important as sight when it comes to detecting slight variations in the drag of an instrument that measures by contact. Experienced mechanics can feel such variations of just a few ten-thousandths of an inch.

The real benefits of electronic digital instruments are felt in industry, because the electronic output can be fed to a computer that forms the heart of a Statistical Process Control (SPC) system. In this way, the dimensions of every part emerging from every machine in a factory can be continuously monitored and their conformance to design specifications ensured automatically. A final advantage of most electronic digital measuring instruments is that they are instantly switchable between inch and metric units.

Some Notes on the Metric System

Perhaps surprisingly, the use of metric weights and measures was made legal by Congress in 1886; the inch/pound system never was! Now called "SI," for "Systéme International"—International System [of Weights and Measures]—it is employed by virtually every country in the world. The only hold-outs are New Guinea, Burma

. . . and the United States! Despite the difficulty of changing the habits of a lifetime, despite the painful and expensive readjustment that will be needed by large parts of American industry, surely it is only a matter of time before the United States goes metric. Accordingly (and because everything mechanical made in the last few decades anywhere outside the United States uses S.I.), a few words about it.

The basic unit of length in the S.I. (metric system) is the *meter*, which has been defined in various ways over the years. Currently, it is defined as the distance light travels in a vacuum during 30.663318 vibrations of a Cesium atom. In practical terms, a meter is about 10 percent more than a yard—39.370079 inches, to be exact.

The meter is, in turn, subdivided into decimeters ("dm"—one-tenth of a meter), centimeters ("cm"—one-hundredth of a meter), and millimeters ("mm"—one-thousandth of a meter), though in practice the decimeter is seldom mentioned. One of the advantages of the metric system is this division of basic units by multiples of 10. It is a considerable rationalization and simplification over multiples of 12, 3, 16, etc.

The basic unit of mass is the *kilogram*, abbreviated as "kg." The

standard is a cylinder of platinum-iridium alloy kept by the International Bureau of Weights and Measures in Paris; a duplicate is kept at the U.S. National Bureau of Standards. (The kilogram is the only basic standard that is still defined by a physical object.) A kilogram, which is approximately equal to 2.2 pounds, is divided into 10 decigrams ("dgm"), 10 centigrams ("cgm"), and 1,000 grams ("gm"). Just as the use of the decimeter is rare, so are the centigram and decigram. Most people who use the metric system would refer to a certain mass as 900 grams, or 0.9 kilogram; terming it 90 centigrams or 9 decigrams, while perfectly correct, would be unusual.

Another convenience of the S.I. is that units of length, mass, and volume are related: One cubic centimeter of pure water weighs one gram; one kilogram of pure water occupies a volume of 1,000 cubic centimeters, which is also defined as one liter ("l"). A liter is just very slightly more than a quart.

For temperature, the S.I. makes use of the Celsius scale, also called Centigrade, abbreviated as "C." The zero point on the Centigrade scale is defined as the freezing point of pure water; the boiling point of water defines 100 on the scale.

Metric Coversion Factors

1 inch (in)	= 25.4 mm (exactly)	1 kilogram (kg)	= 1000 gm
1 foot (ft)	= 304.8 mm (exactly)	1 kilogram (kg)	= 2.205 lb
1 foot (ft)	= 30.48 cm (exactly)	1 cubic inch (cu in)	= 16.387 cc
1 millimeter (mm)	= 0.0394 in	1 cubic centimeter (cc)	= 0.061 cu in
1 centimeter (cm)	= 0.3937 in	1 liter (l)	= 1000 cc
1 meter (m)	= 39.3701 in	1 liter (l)	= 61.024 cu in
1 meter (m)	= 3.2808 ft	1 liter (l)	= 0.264 U.S. gal
1 pound (lb)	= 0.4536 kg	1 U.S. gallon (gal)	= 3.785 l

The Machinist's Rule	 17
The Combination Square	. 20
Outside Calipers	 21
Slide Calipers	 22
Using Slide Calipers	 24
Fixed Gauges	 26
Height Gauges	 27

C
O
N
T
E
N
T
S

While the justification for other more precise and expensive measuring tools depends on the work encountered, every toolbox needs a good rule. Conventional machinist's rules come in various lengths, widths, and thicknesses, in both inch and metric versions. Inch rules may be graduated in simple or decimal fractions, or both. *Mitutoyo/MTI Corporation*

MEASURING A SPAN (PART 1)

In the previous chapter we proposed that, when measuring lengths or distances, the minimum standard for "precision" is an accuracy of 1/10 of 1 percent of the total dimension—1 part in 1,000. In Chapter 3 we will take a look at the use of length-measuring tools that achieve much higher levels of precision and accuracy—1 part in 10,000, or better—but first we will set our sights a little lower.

While a little arithmetic makes it self-evident, it may nevertheless be surprising that "precision," by the above definition, can be achieved with the most basic sort of measuring apparatus, especially when the dimension being measured is comparatively large . . . say, more than a hand-span. And it does not require extremely expensive or elaborate equipment to extend this level of accuracy to

much smaller parts. In historical terms, we are dealing in this chapter with levels of precision (though not necessarily accuracy) attainable by skilled craftsmen of the mid-nineteenth century.

The Machinist's Rule

The oldest and simplest method of measuring the length of an object is to use a rule; common machinist's rules in 6- or 12-inch lengths are likely to be found in most every reader's toolbox. Rules are available up to 12 feet long, but any rule much over 3 feet becomes unwieldy, and tape measures are generally preferred when dealing with greater lengths.

Tape measures are not usually considered as "precision" tools, yet a 30-foot tape only has to be accurate to about 3/8 inch over its full length to have an accuracy of 1 part

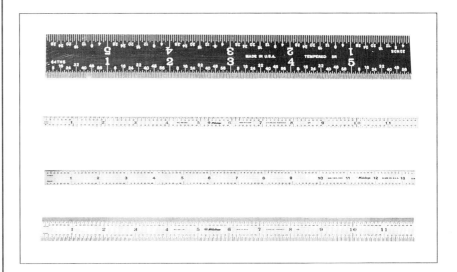

Self-retracting tape measures are limited to about 30 feet in length. When greater lengths need to be accurately measured—laying out a large new shop, surveying a race track—"frame winder" tapes like this are used. They come up to 300 feet in length; 100 foot items are common. *Mitutoyo/MTI Corporation*

per 1,000. About the only other points worth mentioning regarding tapes are, first, that the little hook on the end is loose *on purpose*—the amount of slack is equal to the thickness of the hook, to provide for both inside and outside measurements. People have been known to vigorously wallop the rivets holding the hook on, to "improve" the tool!

Second, when the dimension being measured is large—that is, in the order of umpteen feet, rather than an inch or so—the subject of thermal expansion has to be considered. Steel expands by about 6.5-millionths of an inch per inch for every Fahrenheit degree increase in temperature. The standard reference temperature for measurements is 68 degrees Fahrenheit, so if a tape is used to measure, say, 26 feet 8 inches (320 inches) and the temperature is, say, 98 degrees Fahrenheit, the tape will have grown longer by exactly 1/16 inch. Of course, the thing being measured may also expand, but most things having dimensions measurable in tens of feet are not made of metal. Masonry, for example, has only a fraction of the expansion coefficient of steel.

Finally, there are tapes specifically designed to measure stagger—the difference in size of a pair of rear tires, a matter of great concern to people who race cars with "locked" axles on oval tracks. About the only difference between these and an ordinary carpenter's steel tape is that they are narrower than usual—about 1/4 inch wide—which makes it easier to dodge bits of debris on the tire surface and also reduces the size and weight of the lump in your pocket. A convenience feature on some of these "stagger tapes" is a hook worked to a sharp point, to dig firmly into the tread rubber.

Returning to rules, at the other end of the scale are miniature rules in lengths of 1/4, 3/8, 1/2, 3/4, and 1 inch. These are extremely useful for working in confined spaces or for measuring small inside shoulders, etc. (You can make your own by cutting up an old rule.) They are intended for use with a holder—a knurled handle that clamps to an edge of the rule to permit easy manipulation.

Rules of various lengths are available with a thickness of about 3/64 inch, which makes for a fairly rigid item, or in spring steel of about 1/64-inch thickness, for when a high degree of flexibility is wanted, such as when the rule is carried in a pocket. A width of about 1 inch is common, and provides room for four sets of scales, but narrow rules down to 3/16-inch width, with just one set of markings, are available for use in tight quarters.

Despite the stone-ax simplicity of rules, there are a few points worth dwelling on. First is to consider the level of precision and accuracy that can be achieved. The finest graduation on any steel rule is 1/100 (0.010) inch; rules may be

also be marked in fractions down to 1/64. (Metric rules are invariably marked in one-millimeter or 0.5-millimeter increments, or both.) Few manufacturers lay any particular claim as to the accuracy of their rules, partly, one supposes, because the inherent accuracy of the spacing of the divisions is so much greater than the resolution of the tool that the whole issue becomes almost theoretical. Nevertheless, one maker specifies an accuracy of plus 0.004 inch, minus 0.002 inch, over 6 inches.

It takes good light and a good eye (or a magnifier) to read divisions as small as 1/100 inch, but given those conditions, it appears possible to estimate down to half a division—0.005 inch—or perhaps even less. In fact, we are not nearly as good estimators as we think we are. Rather than reading between the marks, it is wiser to decide which mark is closest, and leave it at that. If a higher level of precision is needed than the resolution of the available scale, get a finer one; if better than 0.01-inch resolution is sought, a tool more inherently precise and accurate than a rule should be used. In any event, the quality of the reading is enhanced if the graduations on the rule are engraved, rather than photo-etched—a properly engraved mark will be V-shaped, more clearly defining the center of the mark.

Unlike ordinary household rules, machinist's rules measure right from the square, machined end; there is no extra margin. This means that it is possible to set the rule dead flush in an inside corner. Nevertheless, it is wise to use the old trick of setting the 1-inch mark, rather than the end of the rule, on the reference point, then subtracting an inch from the final reading. There are three reasons for this: First, while the end of the rule may appear square and true to the unaided eye, it is very likely to be worn or rounded, especially if the rule has been in use for a while. (If this seems excessive nit-picking, examine the zero end of your rule with a 10- or 20-power magnifier.) Second, the edge or corner of the workpiece may not, in fact, be sharp and square. Finally, it is usually more difficult to bring the end or corner of the rule in line with the edge of the work than it is to align one of the graduation marks. "Hook" rules—those having a hardened steel hook at the end—are a convenience in this sort of situation, but it is important to check periodically that the hook has not become worn or loose, and is truly square to the edge of the rule.

Another source of error when using a rule is parallax—the apparent shifting of an object caused by a change in the position of the observer. An example is the error that arises when a passenger attempts to read an automobile speedometer set directly in front of the driver. When measuring with a rule, parallax error can be minimized by setting the rule on edge, rather than laying it flat, and by ensuring that your line of sight is truly at a right angle to the rule and the point you are trying to read.

Apart from plain misreading, the greatest remaining problem is the difficulty of holding the rule still. Even achieving 0.01-inch accuracy with a steel rule *repeatably* usually requires clamping the rule in place—few of us can hold a rule steady within twice that. For work that requires orienting the rule vertically, a purpose-made accessory, called a "rule stand" or "rule holder," allows the rule to project vertically upward relative to the

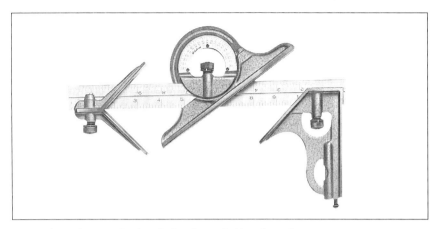

A combination set is the Swiss Army knife of moderate accuracy measurement. It amounts to a combination square—a rule and sliding square head—plus a center head and a protractor head. And like a pocket knife, only one tool is used at a time. *Mitutoyo/MTI Corporation*

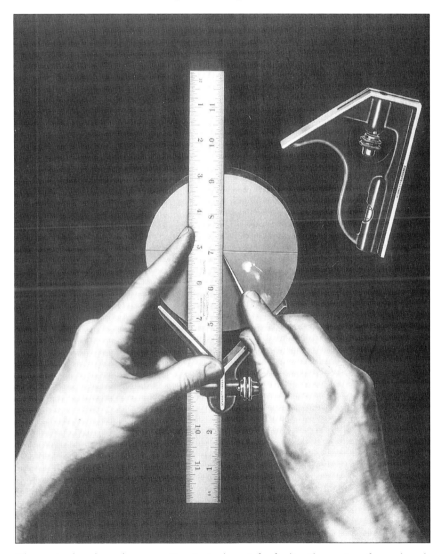

The center head puzzles many. Its principal use is for finding the center of round work (see text), but it can also be used to establish a diagonal line across a square workpiece. *L.S. Starrett Company*

With a skilled sense of touch developed through experience, measurements accurate to a few "thou" can be achieved with something as stone-ax simple as an outside caliper. When the shape of the work prevents withdrawing the tool, calipers with a third transfer leg can be used. *L.S. Starrett Company*

stand base, while holding it still and square.

The Combination Square

A device combining the functions of a rule and a machinist's square was invented in 1877 by Laroy Starrett, founder of the prominent firm of precision instrument makers that bears his name. It comprises a hardened steel rule and a movable square head. The head can be slid along the rule and locked at any position by a lock bolt that engages a groove machined down one face of the rule. Together, they can be used to square a workpiece with a flat surface, to measure a depth, or as a height gauge. The sliding head has a 45 degree face as well as one at 90 degrees to the edge of the rule, permitting checking or laying out angles of 45, 90, and 135 degrees. The usefulness of the device is extended by the addition of a cen-

ter head and a protractor head, plus a scriber, in which case the entire package of rule and accessories is called a "combination set."

We will deal with the use of protractors in Chapter 5, but a few words on the center head may be appropriate here, since people unfamiliar with its use are often puzzled as to its purpose. It could hardly be simpler: It is for finding the center of any round object. The center head has a 90-degree V-shaped opening, aligned so that the edge of the rule exactly bisects the "V." When brought against any circular object so that each of the two legs is touching, the rule automatically lies along a diameter of the circle. After a line has been scribed along this diameter, the tool can be rotated around the shaft about 90 degrees and a second line scribed along this new axis. The two lines will intersect at the exact center of the circle.

A slide caliper is simply a rule with a hook abutment at one end and a sliding head at the other. This "stagger gauge" is a jumbo version, with a twist. Here, the whole unit markings are "pi" inches apart, directly reading-out the entire *circumference* based on a calipering of the *diameter*. It also folds up for convenient storage. *Longacre Automotive Racing Products*

Outside Calipers

It is obviously impossible to directly measure the diameter of a shaft or other circular part using a straight rule. A tool often used in combination with the rule for this and other purposes is a pair of outside calipers. (Traditionally, a single tool is termed a "pair" of calipers, just like a "pair" of trousers.)

These tools come in essentially two types: Those that hold their setting by friction at the joint between the two legs and those that are spring-loaded toward the "big" end of their range with a screw and thumb-nut arrangement to close the calipers against the spring resistance. One variation on the friction joint type provides a thumb-nut to adjust the amount of friction and to permit locking the setting. Finally, for situations where the calipers have to be withdrawn over an obstruction that is larger than the dimension being gauged, there is a version with a third "transfer" leg that can be locked in place. One of the measuring legs can be swung out of the way, and set back against the transfer leg once the tool is free.

Properly used, dial calipers are accurate to about 0.001 inch over 6 inches, the most usual length for these tools. Versions to 12 inches are available. Where slightly submicrometer accuracy is needed over such spans, one such tool can replace several micrometers. *Mitutoyo/MTI Corporation*

Splitting the Difference: The Vernier Scale

It is difficult to describe in words how a Vernier scale "works," but here follows my effort; the adjacent illustrations should help. Typically, the main scale of an inch-reading Vernier caliper is divided into 1/40-inch (0.025) intervals. Twenty-four such divisions, then, span 24 X 0.025 = 0.600 inch.

The Vernier scale, which is attached to the movable jaw, also spans 0.600 inch, but that distance is marked off into 25 equally spaced intervals, not 24—each is 0.024 inch in width. The difference between the width of a single space on the main scale and one on the Vernier scale is thus 0.025 - 0.024 = 0.001 inch, or 1 "thou."

In use, the first part of the reading is made on the main scale. Note how many inches, tenths, and fortieths lie to the left of the zero mark on the Vernier scale. In the illustration, for example, that basic reading is 1.000 plus .400 plus 0.025, or 1.425 inches. Clearly, however, the zero mark on the Vernier scale is "a bit" to the right of the main scale marking indicating 1.425 inches. Establishing just how large that "bit" is the magic of the Vernier scale.

The trick is to find two marks, one on the main scale and one on the Vernier scale, that exactly coincide. In the illustration, the "11" on the Vernier scale lines up exactly with one of the markings on the main scale. Pay no attention to the marking on the main scale, it is the "11" that is important; that 11 gets added to the basic reading, as a number of thousandths. The total, then, is 1.425 + 0.011 = 1.436.

There is more than one way to arrange a Vernier scale. At

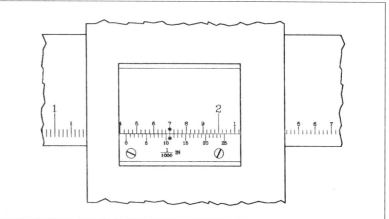

least two manufacturers of precision instruments now offer a "long-scale" Vernier, using 50 graduations on the main scale and 49 on the Vernier scale, rather than the more usual 25 and 24. This spreads the markings out further, allowing easier reading. The Vernier principle is used on a great many measuring tools other than slide calipers, including micrometers, height and depth gauges of various sorts, protractors, etc.

Although seldom encountered, some Verniers are calibrated in simple fractions, rather than decimal fractions; these invariably read to the nearest 1/128 inch. Naturally, there are also metric Verniers, plus instruments that offer both metric and either fractional or decimal inch units. Usually, a metric Vernier scale has 20 divisions, and so reads to 0.05 millimeter. Just as in inch-measuring instruments, however, there are "long scale" metric units that have 50 divisions, reading to 0.02 millimeter.

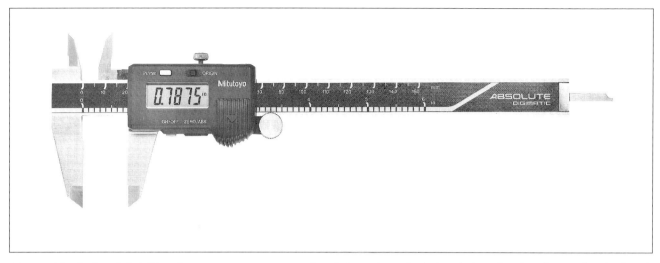

It is arguable whether digital slide calipers are any more accurate than their purely mechanical equivalents, but they do ease the job of reading. Most are also switchable from inch to metric units. *Mitutoyo/MTI Corporation*

As with any other measuring device where one tool is used to gauge an object and the dimension determined by measuring the gauging tool (called, in general, "transfer measurements"), errors can crop up both in the initial gauging and in the subsequent measuring. If the gap of a pair of outside calipers is measured with a rule, the accuracy obviously cannot be greater than that of the rule—0.010 inch, at best. Yet with practice, and a good sense of feel, the initial gauging can be accurate to perhaps 5 "thou," so measuring calipers with a tool more accurate than a rule is justifiable. Alas, this second operation involves an inside measurement and, as we shall detail in Chapter 4, accurately measuring a gap is rather more difficult than measuring a span. For this reason, calipers are best suited for comparison measurements, in which the mechanic's sense of feel is used to judge the difference between the measured span and a reference piece. Calipers come in 6- and 12-inch sizes, the number quoted usually being the straight line distance from the swivel to the points.

Slide Calipers

A slide caliper is simply a rule with a fixed abutment, like a hook rule, plus a sliding head. The head is arranged with a knife edge that crosses the rule exactly in line with the movable jaw, allowing direct reading of the dimension against the rule markings. Usually there is also a means to lock the head, to avoid disturbing the reading when the tool is withdrawn from the work. Such tools still exist, just as described, but while they add convenience (and probably improve repeatability because of the "cursor" function of the sliding jaw), their precision is limited by the resolution of the rule—never finer than 0.010 inch.

A very early modification to the slide caliper that greatly improved its precision was the introduction of the *Vernier scale*, invented by a French mathematician, Pierre Vernier (1580–1637). Although Vernier calipers are now losing popularity to dial and digital calipers, many machinists and mechanics still have a fondness for them. This is partly because they are somewhat more compact (the

dial on dial calipers occasionally gets in the way), and partly because they may have concerns about the accuracy of dial calipers over the long haul (wear of the moving parts over time can potentially introduce some "backlash"). Partly, too, they may simply enjoy exercising an ancient skill that is gradually becoming extinct—see the sidebar "Splitting the Difference."

On inch-measuring dial calipers, the main scale is usually divided into 1/10-inch (0.1) units, while each dial marking represents 0.001 inch; one full revolution of the dial corresponds to one division on the main scale. Beware, however, that you should carefully scope any unfamiliar dial caliper the first time you pick it up: There are some models that use *0.2*-inch units on the main scale. Thus, while a full revolution of the dial still corresponds to one main scale division, those divisions are twice as big. Likewise, each marking on the dial still represents 0.001 inch, but there are twice as many marks.

Metric dial calipers also come in two versions. Perhaps more common is the type with 0.02-millime-

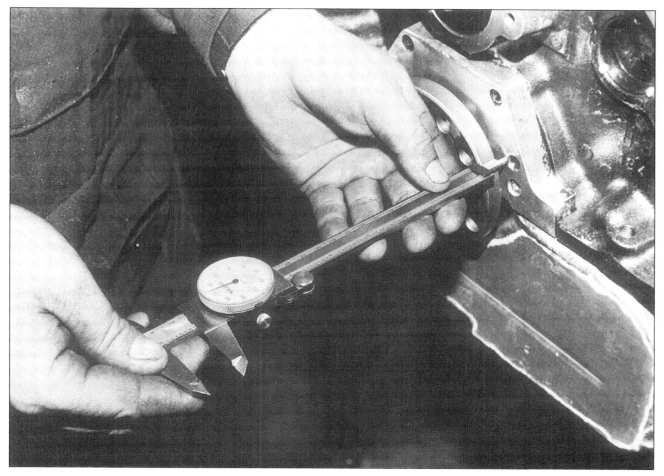

Precision slide calipers—whether dial, digital, or Vernier—are versatile tools. Apart from their considerable range on outside (span) measurements, they can also be used for inside and, as here, for depth measurements. *Doug Gore photo, courtesy* Open Wheel *magazine*

ter divisions on the dial face and in which one full revolution of the pointer corresponds to 2 millimeters. Again, pay attention when handling unaccustomed tools, because there are also versions that have 0.05-millimeter dial divisions with a range of 5 millimeters per revolution, and still others with 0.02-millimeter divisions but with a range of 1 millimeter per rev.

With the exception of some inexpensive "student" models, which read to 0.001 inch or 0.1 millimeter, digital electronic slide calipers seem all to indicate to 0.0005 inch or 0.01 millimeter. Many, too, have the added convenience that they can be "zeroed" at any point, which avoids having to

subtract one measurement from another when comparing two dimensions. Again, with rare exceptions, the read-out can be swapped from inch to metric units at the touch of a button. (Note that some Vernier calipers also have two scales, enabling them to measure in both inch and metric units.)

For all this convenience, note that digital calipers of one popular brand with a resolution of 0.0005 inch have overall accuracy of just 0.001 inch. It seems unwise to offer a measuring instrument that gives a read-out that implies twice the precision of the device's overall accuracy.

Correctly used, quality dial, Vernier, or digital calipers can all

return an accuracy of about 0.001 inch over 6 inches, although the accuracy is likely to diminish over longer spans. One manufacturer lists an accuracy of ± 0.002 inch over 12 inches for its longer-range dial calipers and ± 0.003 inch for both one of its digital models and one of its Vernier calipers, each capable of measuring to 40 (!) inches. Dial calipers are available up to 12 inches, digital ones to 40 inches, and Vernier calipers to 80 inches.

All three types of precision slide calipers are versatile instruments. They provide precision and accuracy approaching that of a micrometer, yet can read dimensions as large as their frame allows.

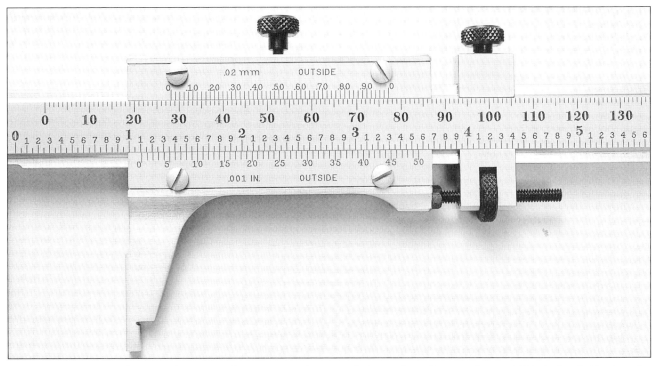

To assist in more accurately setting the gauging force, Vernier calipers usually have a fine-adjustment feature. With the knurled knob at the top right locked, the sliding head is brought into controlled contact with the work using the thumb-wheel at the bottom, and then its position is locked using the other knurled knob. *L.S. Starrett Company*

Micrometer accuracy over more than 3 or 4 inches is rarely needed for the kind of work the average reader of this book is likely to undertake, thus a 6-inch caliper can take the place of several micrometers. They are capable of both outside and inside measurements, and can also be used as depth gauges. Various accessories are available to extend their application and enhance the accuracy of measurements. Precision extension bars can allow an ordinary 6- or 12-inch caliper to measure lengths to 26 inches. A clamp-on T-bar base for depth measurements greatly improves the prospects of getting an accurate reading—always a tricky business. Hole center attachments—cylindrical steel slugs with tapered points—allow directly reading the distances between the centers of two holes.

Using Slide Calipers

Once a worker is familiar with his own precision slide calipers, of whatever type, an incorrect measurement resulting from misreading is much less likely than one resulting from improper handling of the tool. One respect in which slide calipers are inherently inferior to micrometers is that there is no means of controlling the force applied to the jaws of the tool when measuring. Obviously the jaws, cantilevered outboard of the scale as they are, will "spring" somewhat whenever a force is applied to them. To obtain repeatable results, the force applied during a measurement must be held as consistent as possible from one use to the next.

The use of precision slide calipers is pretty much a two-handed job. The fixed jaw end of the caliper should be supported in the

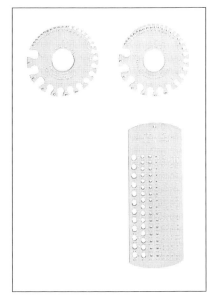

Drill gauges (below) are found in most shops; wire and sheet gauges (above) are perhaps less common. In certain size ranges, the steps between different drill and wire diameters are small enough to allow these simple, inexpensive tools to be used to gauge the diameter of round work with surprising precision. *Mitutoyo/MTI Corporation*

Stone Simple: The Surface Plate

Once the needed level of precision exceeds that of a machinist's rule, every measurement of a span involves contacting the part being measured at two points. In the case of calipers of all sorts, including micrometers, discussed in the next chapter, the two contact points are part of the measuring tool itself. In other cases, such as the height gauge (next page) and the dial indicator (Chapter 3), the tool only has one point of contact with the work. Nevertheless, a second point of contact is needed. That second contact point is usually the spot where the "other" side of the work touches a reference surface. Purpose-made reference surfaces are called surface plates.

At one time, surface plates were commonly made of cast iron, ground and lapped to a very high degree of flatness and smoothness. Iron surface plates had the advantage that work or measuring tools could be secured to them magnetically, but they also had some drawbacks. First, iron rusts, and even the slightest amount of corrosion would disrupt both the flatness and the smoothness of a surface plate. Second, there was the problem of scratches on the surface. While any material can be scratched, even very hard metals retain some "plasticity"—they behave a bit like high-strength putty. So when an iron plate is scratched, there is not only a furrow in the surface, material also gets "heaped up" on either side of the trough, like soil turned aside by a plow. Whatever rested on top would end up perched on those raised ridges that might amount to several "tenths." Still, in my view, an old iron plate in good shape is just fine . . . if you can find one!

The material of choice these days is granite. Granite is dimensionally stable, at least twice as hard as cast iron, and does not rust. What is more, scratches simply leave grooves, with no buildup of material outboard of the scratch. Apart from the arguable drawback that it is non-magnetic, about the only respect in which a granite plate is inferior to an iron one is that the dull surface makes it almost impossible to use an optical flat (see the sidebar "Seeing Double" in Chapter 3) to check the surface for wear. Granite surface plates come in sizes from about 12 by 18 inches, to units measuring 6 by 12 feet. Smaller versions, down to 8 by 12 inches, are offered, sometimes called "toolmakers flats."

Variation from flatness is controlled and defined by federal specifications. Just as with gauge blocks, various grades are available. Laboratory "AA" grade plates of small-to-medium size are flat within 0.00005 over their entire area; "inspection" and "shop" grades within 0.0001 and 0.0002 inch, respectively. The thickness of a surface plate is set in proportion to its outside dimensions so that a 50-pound load applied in the middle of the plate does not deform it more than half of the flatness tolerance.

When setting up a surface plate, it is obviously advantageous to arrange for it to be dead level in both planes. Apart from the general usefulness of having at least one thing in the shop that is definitely flat and level, any significant slope to the surface will introduce a different "feel" when sliding an instrument such as a height gauge "uphill" versus "downhill," leading to mistaken judgments about the comparative heights of things. If nothing else, ensuring that a surface plate is truly level will prevent things from rolling off it!

Use extreme care when setting measuring instruments or work on the plate; although hard, granite is brittle, so it is not especially difficult to chip or gouge the surface. Above all, keep the plate covered when it's not in use; a sort of inverted shallow wooden box that completely surrounds the plate is best. And certainly do not let the plate become used as a general-purpose work surface; tools, coffee cups, etc., do not belong. A granite plate can be cleaned with ordinary soap and water.

A final word: so-called "plate glass" has sometimes been used as a "poor man's" surface plate. Indeed, plate glass can be ground so that its surface varies in height by not more than ten-millionths of an inch. Trouble is, nobody makes plate glass anymore; what is sold as "plate glass" is, in fact, "float glass." While this stuff looks perfectly flat, the variation in thickness over a modest area is typically no less than 0.006 inch. Forget it.

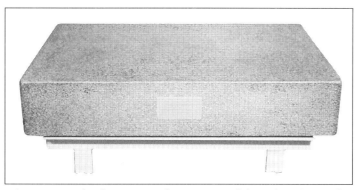

When gauging the flatness, straightness, or parallelism of *anything*, a flat reference surface is mighty handy. Purpose-made ones are called surface plates. Once they were made of ground and lapped cast iron, but granite is now the preferred material. While surface plates and height gauges make a natural pairing, countless measuring tasks are made easier when a plane known to be flat and level is on hand. Some are impossible without one. *Mitutoyo/MTI Corporation*

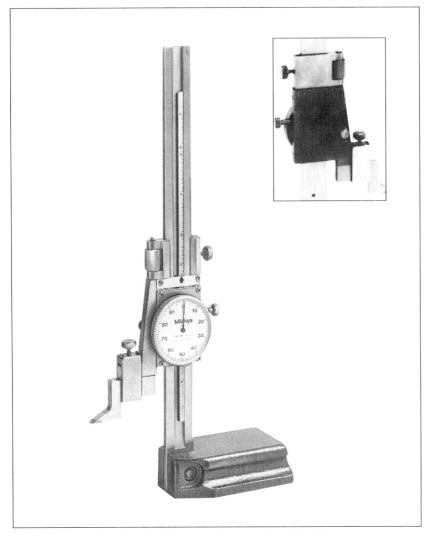

Height gauges can be thought of as vertically oriented precision slide calipers, with the fixed jaw missing. That function is served by the surface the gauge rests on, usually a surface plate. Often considered as machine shop equipment, the combination of a surface plate and a height gauge fitted with a test indicator is in fact a versatile, general purpose dimensional gauging device. *Mitutoyo/MTI Corporation*

left hand, the sliding jaw in the other. You should not hold the tool by the main rule extending beyond the jaws. The fixed jaw should always be set against the work to be measured first, then the sliding jaw moved in until solid contact is made. Just how "solid" is more difficult to say. One way the appropriate force has been expressed is that it should be about the same as that used to press on a pencil when writing.

Once you think you have the

tool straight and square with the work and you believe the contact pressure is correct, use the clamping screw (they all have one) to lock the reading. Before actually taking that reading, test the "feel" of the calipers against the work; the narrow knife-edge on the jaws makes it very easy to slightly misjudge the squareness with the work. On outside measurements, this will always take the form of the reading being "high"; any error in positioning will reveal itself as some slight

looseness when the correct position is achieved.

The most precise type of Vernier calipers involves an extra step, arising from the provision on these tools of a fine adjustment, intended specifically to help minimize this problem of centering the tool on the work. With these, after making contact with the sliding jaw, back it off ever so slightly and secure the locking screw for the main adjustment. Then use the fine adjustment to again bring the movable jaw into contact and, when you believe you have the positioning and force correct, lock the fine adjustment. Now go through the "feel" test again, and if necessary, unlock the fine adjustment and have another go at it.

Fixed Gauges

In mass production work, various single-purpose fixed gauges are used to check a part's dimensions. For checking the outside diameter of round work, these usually take the form of a pair of rings, a big one, called the "GO" gauge and a smaller one, the "NO-GO" gauge. An inspector can thus simply slip the part into the gauge (or the gauge onto the part). As long as the part fits within the "GO" gauge but will not pass through the "NO-GO" gauge, then he knows that the dimension is smaller than the maximum permissible but larger than the minimum.

This sort of fixed gauge probably has no place in the average auto enthusiast's tool kit, but there are some other fixed gauges that do. Most common among these is a drill or wire gauge, which is simply a flat, hardened steel plate with a number of precisely sized holes in it. Drill bits come in fractional inch, number series, letter series, and metric sizes. Likewise, there are various standards for wire diameters, including U.S. Standard Gauge (USG), Brown & Sharpe wire gauge (B&S), Birmingham Wire Gauge (BWG), and others.

Considering all these various "standards" together, the steps are often very close together over a wide and useful range of diameters. Thus, someone armed only with a small assortment of drill and wire gauges, and using them as "GO/NO-GO" gauges, can pin down the diameter of a piece of rod stock of unknown size with surprising precision. For example, 15/64 inch is 0.234 inch, while 6 millimeters is 0.236 inch; similarly, an "S" drill is 0.348 inch, while 11/32 inch is 0.344. Again, No. 18 BWG is 0.049 inch, while No. 18 USG is 0.050 inch. Clearly, in some cases it is possible to achieve "precision," by our definition, with a ridiculously cheap and simple tool.

Height Gauges

A height gauge consists of a vertical bar equipped with a precision rule supported on an integral base, together with a sliding head equipped with a Vernier or dial reading to (usually) 0.001 inch. The base is ground and lapped to a very high finish and is dead square to the vertical bar. Bars up to 48 inches are available (and even longer on special order), but 12- or 24-inch heights are more usual.

Height gauges are most often found in machine shops, where they are commonly used for layout work, rather than in automotive shops. For layout work, the sliding head is equipped with a hardened scriber. With the height gauge rest-

ing on a surface plate (see sidebar), or other smooth and truly flat surface, lines can thus be scribed on a workpiece at exact known heights above the surface plate. The tool can also be used directly for measurement, in which role it offers an accuracy of about 0.001 inch per foot. One application, for example, might be measuring the deck height of an engine block during "blueprinting," and determining whether this dimension is uniform from end-to-end.

Considerably greater accuracy than 0.001 inch can be achieved, on *comparative* measurements, by fitting a dial test indicator (see Chapter 3) in place of the scriber. When using the height gauge, it is important that the tool be slid around on the reference surface only by its base; dragging it around by the vertical bar can disturb the accuracy of the squareness of the bar to the base. It should also be moved *slowly*, otherwise there may be a tendency for the base to "chatter" across the surface, which can damage either the base or the surface plate. And it seems hardly necessary to say that dropping the gauge will surely trash its accuracy, if not destroy the tool completely.

It is hard to exaggerate the importance of caring for the undersurface of the base, which is finished to near gauge block flatness. Dragging the base over an edge or corner of a surface plate, or moving it around on a surface that has dirt or grit on it, can severely impair its flatness . . . to say nothing of the surface plate. When out of use, the gauge should be returned to its storage box.

C O N T E N T S

The Micrometer Caliper . . 29

Reading a Micrometer . . . 31

The Vernier Micrometer . 32

Reading a Vernier
Micrometer 34

The Use of Micrometers . 34

The Dial Indicator 38

Use of the Dial Indicator . 41

Dial Test Indicators 43

Gauge Blocks 44

MEASURING A SPAN (PART 2)

Provided you weren't too fussy about just exactly whose "inch" you were working with, by the 1850s it was possible, using a Vernier caliper with care, to measure with a precision approaching 0.001 inch, and this was ample for most engineering purposes. Still, there were some areas of manufacturing—watch-making, for example—where 1 thou was at the bottom edge of acceptability.

The device that allowed a consistently higher order of precision than that offered by the Vernier caliper, and one that demanded a little less of the user, was the micrometer. The Vernier caliper, in widespread use for precision work by the mid-1800s, was invented about 1640; the principle of the micrometer had been invented about the same time, but it took nearly 200 years for that principle to be applied to a practical, hand-held tool.

The origin of the "mike," as it is often abbreviated in speech, can be attributed to a French astronomer, Gascoigne, who fitted his telescope with a pair of indicators that could be opened and closed by a screw thread to measure the size of the image in the eyepiece and so establish the size of the object viewed. Obviously, a minuscule error in gauging the size of the image could result in an enormous error in the estimate of the diameter of the object, and Gascoigne knew that it would be impossible to measure the gap in his indicator with sufficient accuracy, using a rule.

So, Gascoigne counted the number of whole and fractional turns of the screw that it took to open a gap that exactly spanned the image. Then, having established the number of threads per inch of the screw thread, he applied a little mathematics to convert that count into a dimension. Two hundred years later, in 1848, another Frenchman, Palmer, developed Gascoigne's device into the forerunner of the modern micrometer. Palmer used Gascoigne's screw thread, but eliminated the mathematics by engraving a series of fine lines on both the fixed and moving parts of the tool that made it possible to read the dimensions directly, without the need for calculations.

At the Paris Exposition in 1867, American businessmen J.R. Brown and Lucian Sharpe saw Palmer's device on display. Impressed, they returned to the United States to introduce the "Pocket Sheet Metal Gage" [sic]. This first micrometer caliper capable of reading in thousandths of an inch was useful, but had some drawbacks. For one thing, the screw thread was exposed, and so liable to damage and contamination. In 1890, Laroy Starrett patented an improved micrometer that enclosed the thread within a tubular sleeve, and that had a slimmed-down body to fit into tight quarters. Starrett

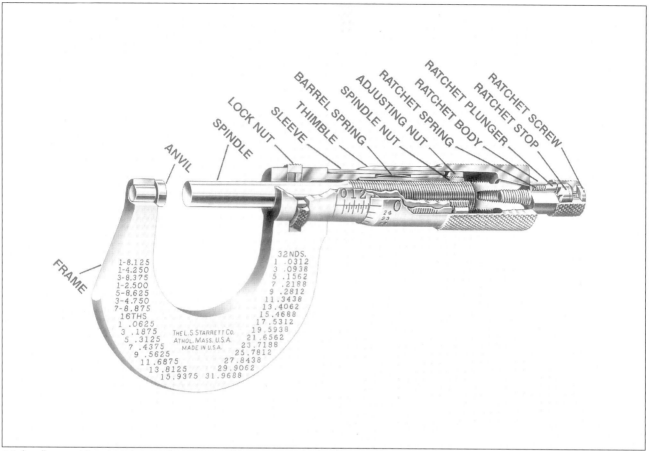

It is hardly surprising that the two firms responsible, respectively, for the introduction and for the modernization of the micrometer are now the two leading precision tool companies in the United States—Brown & Sharpe and L.S. Starrett Co. The modern micrometer caliper combines the two-point contact of a slide caliper with a precision screw adjustment that allows highly accurate measurement. *L.S. Starrett Company*

also provided a small, knurled thumb wheel at the end of the screw as a "speeder," to take some of the drudgery out of closing the micrometer onto the workpiece, and arranged for a locking device, to hold the reading. This is the tool we recognize today as the most accurate hand-held measuring tool available.

The Micrometer Caliper

The heart of the micrometer is a shaft or *spindle* having a hardened precision screw thread over part of its length. The screw thread is engaged with an equally precise nut secured in one end of a "C"-shaped frame. Turning the screw thus causes it to move toward or away from the other end of the "C"-frame, which has a precisely flat fixed abutment, or *anvil*. The screw is surrounded by a stationary sleeve attached to the frame, which both protects the screw and has a series of marks engraved along its length. Also surrounding the screw, and attached to it, is a barrel or *thimble*, which has lines engraved around its perimeter.

On inch-measuring micrometers, the screw thread conventionally has a pitch of 40 threads to the inch, thus each full turn of the screw advances it 1/40 (0.025) inch toward the anvil. The sleeve has a corresponding mark engraved every 0.025 inch, usually with every fourth mark (corresponding to 0.100 inch) numbered. The marks on the perimeter of the thimble divide its circumference into 25 parts, thus each mark corresponds to 0.001 inch of spindle travel. (Metric measuring micrometers have a screw with a pitch of 0.5 millimeter, so 50 full turns of the screw advance it 25 millimeters. The thimble has 50 graduations, so each mark corresponds to 0.01 millimeter of spindle travel).

The most common size of micrometer is the familiar 1-inch model, but larger sizes are available, up to 24 inches, and in some cases to 40(!) inches. However, because the sleeve-and-nut assembly is

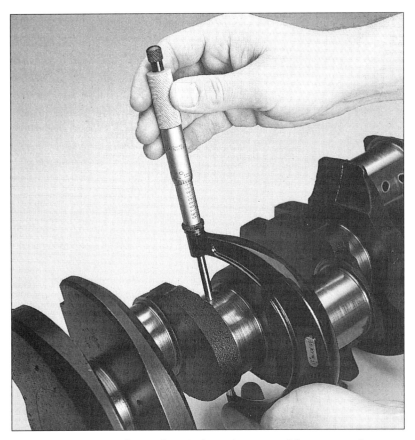

While most micrometers have only a 1-inch travel, some special-purpose versions span a wider range. This automotive crankshaft micrometer from Starrett measures from 1 1/2 to 3 1/2 inches. The reading line and sleeve markings are also moved to the underside of the tool, to ease reading. *L.S. Starrett Company*

While micrometers with rounded anvils are available for measuring tubing and the like, in which flat contact surfaces would "bridge" over the inside of the work, a general-purpose micrometer can be used there if a round spacer, such as a ball bearing, is set against the anvil. Fumbling and the need for a third hand are eliminated by this adapter that holds the ball onto the anvil. *Brown & Sharpe, North Kingston, RI*

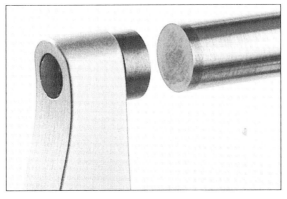

Where abrasive conditions exist, tungsten carbide contact surfaces on spindle tip and anvil greatly increase the life span of a micrometer, but this material cannot be finished quite as smoothly as conventional, lapped and polished steel surfaces. Some people believe the conventional contacts have superior "feel." *L.S. Starrett Company*

overhung from the frame, there are practical limitations on the length of that assembly, so each separate size of "mike" usually only spans a 1-inch range. Thus, a "2-inch" micrometer measures from 1 inch to 2 inches, a "3-inch" model from 2 to 3 inches, etc. To permit one of these larger micrometers to measure objects smaller than its closed dimension, some are available with interchangeable anvils, in 1-inch increments of length. Also, some makers offer an accessory "shoe" for a 2-inch mike that fits over the existing fixed anvil, to allow it to measure from zero to 1 inch. Although much less common, there are some micrometers with 2-inch travel. One such instrument is a special-purpose tool made by Starrett. With a span from 1 1/2 to 3 1/2 inches, it is intended specifically for measuring automotive crankshaft journals. There are also mikes with 1/4- or 1/2-inch travel, for situations in which a reduced overall size is more important than a wide working range.

For specialized work, micrometers are available with differently shaped anvils and spindles. When measuring the wall thickness of tubing, for instance, a flat anvil would bridge across the curvature of the inside of the tube, giving an erroneous reading. For this sort of work, micrometers with a rounded rather than flat anvil may be used. As an alternative to having separate micrometers for various types of measurement, makers of these tools also offer adapters that slip on to the anvil to convert it from a flat to a rounded surface. These basically amount to a precision steel ball in a retainer that allows one side of the ball to contact the anvil, leaving the opposite side exposed for contact with the work. A precision bearing ball can obviously be used by itself as a spacer. In either case, the diameter of the ball is then subtracted from the final reading. Anvils and spindles with pointed contacts are available for measuring screw threads.

Carbide anvils and spindle tips are offered by most manufacturers of micrometers, and these will surely wear longer than the ordinary steel type, especially if, say, you are frequently gauging parts that are being ground, where some abrasive from the grinding may cling to the workpiece. Still, some experienced craftsmen believe they get a better "feel" with the traditional, highly polished steel contacts.

Frames with shapes other than the familiar "C" are sometimes encountered. A shallow, low-profile frame is used, for example, to reach inside holes and other recesses, to measure, say, the thickness of an internal flange. These are sometimes called "hub" micrometers. Conversely, there are deep-throat models, for measuring thickness at a substantial distance inboard of an edge. Note, too, that just as the Vernier principle is used for measuring tools other than calipers, the micrometer principle also crops up in assorted other applications; we will later discuss several of these. In every case, however, the use and reading are essentially the same as for the familiar 1-inch "mike."

Reading a Micrometer

To read an inch-measuring micrometer, first note that the markings on the stationary sleeve are arranged along a "reading" or "witness" line. Each marking across that line represents 0.025 inch of spindle travel; customarily, every fourth mark (that is, every 0.1 inch) is numbered. The edge of the thimble is also marked with divisions, 25

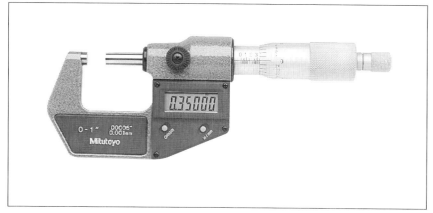

Digital electronic micrometers ease reading, especially compared to a Vernier micrometer, and especially for beginners, but are generally no more accurate than a mechanical Vernier type. They are, however, significantly more expensive. *Mitutoyo/MTI Corporation*

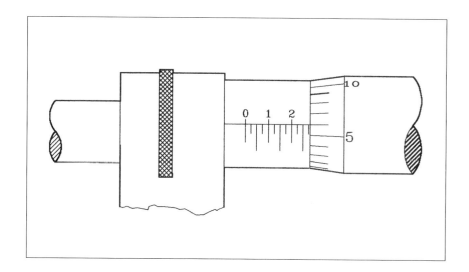

of them in total, thus each mark represents 1/25 of a turn of the thimble and screw, or 0.001 inch.

First, observe the last number exposed on the sleeve, and note that value as "tenths." In the adjacent illustration, for example, the number "2" is visible, so the value to record is 0.200. Then count up the number of lines on the sleeve between the "2" and the edge of the thimble; in the illustration there are three such additional lines. Since each line represents 0.025, the total is 3 x 0.025 = 0.075. Next, note which line on the edge of the

thimble coincides with the reading line. In the illustration, the line is the sixth one after the zero on the thimble. Each line on the thimble represents 0.001, so six of them make 0.006. Finally, add up the three separate values: 0.200 + 0.075 + 0.006 = 0.281.

A fairly common problem in reading a micrometer is a tendency to misread the number of 0.025-inch division lines on the sleeve, especially if a line is very near the edge of the thimble and the light is poor. About the only sure fix for this is to "back up"

Seeing Double: Optical Flats and Parallels

A device called an "optical flat" can be used to check the flatness of critical surfaces, such as the anvil and spindle surfaces of a micrometer. A similar item, an "optical parallel," can do the same and can also establish their parallelism. Each consists of a chunk of optical glass, quartz, or Pyrex™ which, when set on a nominally flat surface, reveals variations from true flatness by a means called optical interferometry—the interference of light waves.

To explain, transparent substances, by definition, allow light waves to travel through them. But not all the light gets through; some of it reflects off the outside surface before it even enters (this is what you are seeing when a piece of glass glints in the sun), and some reflects off the inside of the opposite surface before it makes it out the far side.

Thus, if a flat piece of glass is laid against a reasonably flat reflective surface, such as a machined metal part, light will travel through the glass, bounce off the shiny metal surface, and travel back through the glass in the opposite direction. Some of the light that enters, however, will not make it all the way to the reflective surface beneath; it will reflect off the interior of the glass surface instead. So, there are two reflections—one from the shiny metal surface, and one from the interior of the far surface of the glass.

Obviously, if the glass is truly flat but the metal surface is not, these two reflections will have different starting points, separated by the thickness of the wedge-shaped air space that exists because one edge of the glass is propped up by some microscopic irregularity of the metal surface. Now, light acts like waves, so if a light is shone through the setup described above, the two sets of waves with different starting points will be out of step with each other, in some places completely canceling each other out. This reveals itself as a series of dark "interference bands," or "fringes," visible through the viewing side of the glass. In daylight, a single interference band results from an air gap thickness (and thus a variation from flatness) of about 0.00001 inch.

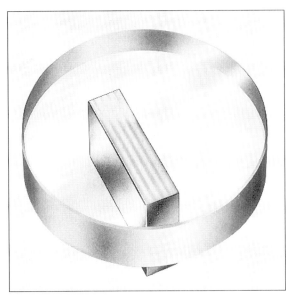

Any variation from dead flatness of a smooth machined surface can be visualized, and quantified to some extent, using an optical flat—a piece of quartz or Pyrex™ glass ground flat within one- to four-millionths of an inch, according to make and grade. A visible dark band appears for approximately every ten-millionths of an inch tilt of the glass on the surface; curved and otherwise distorted bands reveal localized dips and peaks. *Photo courtesy L.S. Starrett Company.*

It seems that all the optical flats available these days are circular, ranging in diameter from about 1 inch to 12 inches, and from 1/2 inch to 2 inches in thickness. The precision surface is flat to within at least five-millionths of an inch, and in some cases to one-millionth. Optical parallels are flat on both surfaces to comparable accuracy and the surfaces are parallel to each other to twenty- millionths or better; some are guaranteed to be parallel within four-millionths.

Sets of four parallels in carefully planned increments of thickness offer an interesting alternative to a set of micrometer-checking gauge blocks. They serve very much the same purpose as the blocks but also allow the visual checking of micrometer anvils and spindle tips for flatness and parallelism. The only potential problem here is the likelihood of causing scratches on the surface of the parallels, especially if the micrometer is equipped with carbide contacts. This is a minor consideration, however—a modest amount of scratching will not impair the dimensional gauging function, as it has to be quite severe before the fringes became unreadable, and it takes considerable use before this occurs. And even if one area of a parallel becomes spoiled in this way, lots more area is available—and there are always the other three.

A standard 1-inch micrometer is designed to be held and manipulated with one (right) hand, leaving the other hand free to hold the object being measured. (Lefties are out of luck!) *Mitutoyo/MTI Corporation*

until all doubt is removed about the position of the line, then *slowly* reapproach the final reading, while keeping track of the zero mark on the thimble.

The Vernier Micrometer

Only very rarely does a line on the thimble exactly coincide with the witness line on the sleeve. Accordingly, and given that the spaces between the marks on a micrometer thimble are rather wide—about 1/16 inch—it is tempting to "eyeball" an estimated value between marks. We repeat here our caution against this.

Not all manufacturers publish accuracy specifications for their 1-inch mechanical micrometers, but those that do invariably claim an accuracy of 0.0001 inch or better. What is needed to break a 1 "thou" division down into smaller parts, then, is not greater accuracy but finer resolution. As with slide

calipers, the solution is to provide micrometers with a Vernier scale. (Although both Vernier calipers and the rudimentary micrometer existed in the mid-nineteenth century, it was not until the early 1920s that the Vernier micrometer first appeared.)

Vernier micrometers have an additional set of lines engraved on the sleeve that, viewed together with the 1-thou markings on the thimble, provide the Vernier feature. These lines run parallel to the witness line; if you imagine holding the mike in your right hand with the "C" of the frame at the bottom, as you would for a typical measurement, the Vernier scale is located on the "top" of the sleeve. Ten of these division lines occupy the same space as nine division lines on the thimble, and it is this 1-part-in-10 difference between the spacing of the two sets of markings that allows for reading with a precision of 0.0001 inch.

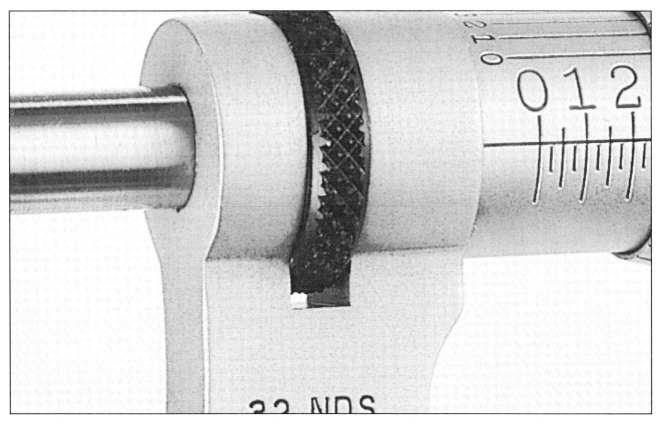

It is generally preferable, and sometimes necessary, to withdraw the micrometer from the work before taking a reading from it. A lock ring is provided that clamps a split collet onto the spindle threads, to avoid disturbing the setting. *L.S. Starrett Company*

Reading a Vernier Micrometer

The first step in reading a Vernier mike is to establish the dimension to the nearest thousandth, in the same way described above for a "regular" micrometer. Then examine the Vernier scale to see which of these extra lines on the sleeve coincide with a marking on the thimble. The number identifying that line on the Vernier scale indicates the additional number of "tenths" that have to be added to the basic reading. The adjacent illustrations should make this clear.

Again, as with a Vernier caliper, the important thing to remember is that it is the number on the *Vernier* scale that matters. Pay no attention to which line on the sleeve is involved—it only serves as a pointer.

We should emphasize here that one ten-thousandth of an inch is a very small dimension indeed—about 1/30 the diameter of a human hair—and it takes very little to affect the accuracy of a measurement with that level of apparent precision. A 15-degree temperature rise will cause a 1-inch chunk of steel to grow by 0.0001 inch; the difference between typical room temperature and human body temperature will thus account for a two "tenths" difference over 1 inch. Below, we discuss some of the other factors that affect the accuracy of a micrometer.

The Use of Micrometers

The accuracy of a micrometer is affected by a number of factors, including the flatness and parallelism of the anvil and spindle contact surfaces, the accuracy of the screw pitch, distortion of the frame, and the accuracy of the engraved markings on the thimble and sleeve. Assuming the tool is from a reputable manufacturer, and

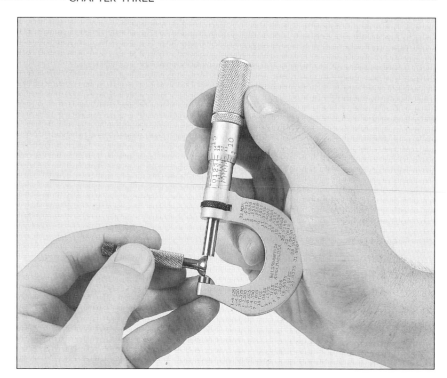

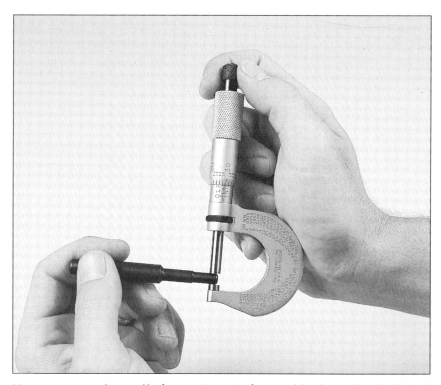

You can get any reading you like from a micrometer if you crank hard enough on the knurled thimble—the frame will spring open. To achieve accuracy, a controlled gauging force is needed. Two means to achieve this are a slip-clutch built into the thimble (top) or a ratchet mechanism attached to the speeder knob. *L.S. Starrett Company*

has not been grossly abused (I wasn't kidding about that ignition wrench story), we can pretty much discount any problems arising from the frame or screw or engravings. But the anvil and spindle faces can become worn, damaged, or simply covered with grunge. It is entirely practical to check a micrometer's contact surfaces yourself (see the sidebar "Seeing Double"), but an instrument that has been well cared for is more likely to give a false reading because of dirt, rather than physical damage.

There will almost certainly be a thin film of oil on the gauging surfaces of any micrometer. Now, that film is almost infinitesimally thin and will not, by itself, upset the accuracy of the instrument. But oil is a magnet for dust and it is easy for a buildup of grime on the anvil and spindle point to accumulate to several "thou" in thickness. To ensure against errors from this cause, cautious craftsmen clean the contact surfaces of the anvil and spindle prior to every use. Simply close the spindle onto the anvil, using light pressure, with a clean piece of paper in between; then pull the paper out. Afterward, open the jaws slightly and blow any paper lint off the sharp edges of the contacting surfaces. You should try to avoid touching the gauging surfaces of the anvil and spindle with your bare hand—sweat is acidic and can cause corrosion. And it should be obvious that the work to be measured also has to be scrupulously clean.

If what is being measured is a small, loose piece—a small part, a small-hole gauge (see Chapter 4), etc.—the tool should be held in the right hand, with a couple of fingers curled around the "C"-frame, leaving the thumb and forefinger free to turn the thimble, while the

workpiece or gauge is held in the left hand. However, if the object to be measured is not readily portable, then the mike has to be brought to the work. In that case, it will probably prove easiest to hold the frame of the mike in the left hand.

In every case, as with slide calipers, the fixed anvil should be brought into contact with the work first, then the thimble rotated to bring the spindle into contact. Also as with slide calipers, the spindle should be locked and the tool manipulated gently to ensure that it has not been "cocked" off at an angle. The width of the anvil and spindle surfaces is appreciable compared to the usual knife edge contacts of a slide caliper, so errors arising from this sort of misalignment are less likely. Still, bear in mind that the edges of a micrometer's contact surfaces are sharp, and it is quite possible to "dig a corner in" and be unaware of it.

Another possible source of error when using a mike is closing the spindle onto the work too quickly; the approach should be slow, to aid in achieving a consistent gauging force on every measurement. Although their sturdier frames mean that micrometers "spring" less than slide calipers, a uniform, controlled contact force is still needed to achieve repeatable readings. A considerable aid to accuracy, then, is a means to establish that controlled gauging force.

Apart from investing the time necessary to gain an expert "touch," there are two approaches to this. First is a simple friction clutch built into the thimble that slips when a certain, appropriate amount of torque is applied. The other arrangement involves a ratchet mechanism built into the "speeder" knob at the end of the thimble. If the spindle is tightened onto the

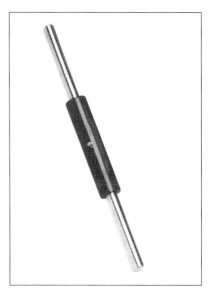

A micrometer standard is a piece of steel rod produced to a precise length with ends ground as flat and as parallel as the contact surfaces on a micrometer. They are used to check the zero adjustment on outside micrometers larger than 1-inch. Problems of thermal expansion increase as the length becomes greater (as here, on a 6-inch standard), so insulated hand grips are provided. *Mitutoyo/MTI Corporation*

work using the speeder, the ratchet will similarly govern the firmness of the contact force. This latter scheme leaves the thimble solidly connected to the spindle, and some workers prefer this as it provides the option of gauging by manual "feel." Still, the choice between these two designs is largely a matter of personal preference; most makers offer a choice.

With the contact surfaces clean, the mike should read zero when the spindle is brought into contact with the anvil with normal gauging force. (A ratchet or friction thimble virtually eliminates variability here.) If it does not, you can add or subtract the amount of the discrepancy on every measurement or else (and preferably) adjust the instrument. This procedure is quite simple, but differs from make-to-make, so we will not be describing it here. Every micrometer sold new comes with detailed instructions for this; if you have lost the paperwork, contact the manufacturer.

It is good practice to check a micrometer for accuracy from time to time, or before using it for a critical task. Very accurately made measuring rods called "micrometer standards" are available, although these invariably come in exact 1-inch increments of length and are most commonly used to check the zero setting on micrometers larger than 1 inch. (Thus, a 1-inch standard confirms the 1-inch point on a 1-inch mike and the zero point on a 2-inch unit.) Sets comprising a small number of gauge blocks are available, specifically for checking micrometers.

The instrument should be checked at various settings, especially including near its maximum size. It might seem reasonable that a 1-inch mike should also be checked at, say, 1/4, 1/2, and 3/4, but these dimensions correspond to *full turns* of the screw, and so they may not reveal certain kinds of repetitive errors in the pitch of the screw threads. Meticulous craftsmen prefer a more random selection of checking lengths, and the sets of gauge blocks offered for micrometer-checking take this into account.

Apart from the dimensional accuracy of the object used to calibrate a mike, there is the issue of its shape. To explain, first understand that the user does not really have direct control over the gauging

Dial indicators report the movement of the contact foot on a clock-like face. In view of the numerous possible forms of display, each printed *number* on the face indicates 0.001 inch (on inch-measuring units), whatever the resolution suggested by the *lines*. This is a "balanced" dial, with positive values on the right side and negative values on the left. Note the "9 o'clock" rest position of the hand; pre-loading the instrument to zero eliminates backlash around the zero mark. *Federal Products Co.*

The clock-work heritage of dial indicators is apparent inside as well as out. Here we can clearly see how linear movement of the plunger is converted to rotary motion by a rack-and-pinion mechanism, then that motion amplified by a train of "step-up" gears. Jeweled bearings, another feature of quality clocks and watches, reduce friction, add to instrument life. *Federal Products Co.*

force applied between the micrometer contacts and the workpiece—he (or the friction thimble or ratchet) only really controls the *torque* applied to the thimble. Because the spindle of a micrometer rotates, there is some slight rotary "scrub" between it and the check piece, and so some frictional resistance. It is actually that friction which is detected, whether by the technician or the friction clutch.

Now, when the flat gauging surfaces of a micrometer are closed against a flat surface, such as a gauge block, the contact extends over the full area of the anvil and spindle tip. But when a round workpiece is checked, the contact takes place only over an almost infinitely thin line or, in the case of a ball, a point. In this latter case, the frictional "scrub" will be greatly reduced, so the friction thimble or ratchet will permit more spindle travel before breaking loose. Thus, a micrometer checked against a flat reference piece will tend to read very slightly low when used to measure round work; similarly, one checked against a round check piece, then used to measure flat work, will read very slightly high. From decades of experience, micrometer manufacturers have determined that this discrepancy can amount to about 0.0001 inch.

This possible inaccuracy can be eliminated by using alternative calibration standards consisting of short lengths of hard, round steel wirestock of known, accurate diameters. Oddly, while all micrometer makers offer micrometer-checking sets of gauge blocks (having flat surfaces), none sell reference standards of circular shape. They leave this highly specialized business to the numerous companies specializing in precision wire products.

Among dial indicators, anything more than about 0.250 inch is considered "long range." Contrast the "continuous reading" dial on this 1-inch model with the "balanced" dial seen previously. When the combination of precision and range of the instrument means the pointer rotates more than the usual 2 1/4–2 1/3 revolutions, an auxiliary counter is usually provided to keep track of the total number of turns. *Federal Products Co.*

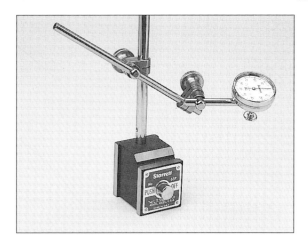

A magnetic base is a most useful accessory for a dial indicator, here seen holding a "back plunger" type of indicator. Clamps, or "snugs," permit orienting the indicator at almost any angle relative to the base. To reduce spring and flex in the setup, all overhangs of the support rods should be kept to a minimum. *L.S. Starrett Company*

Quite minor variations in the gauging force can also produce errors of a tenth or more; there is good reason to be skeptical of any measurement to a tenth precision taken without using the friction thimble or ratchet speeder. All this, plus the previously mentioned effects of even modest temperature changes, hints at the need for being very conservative and cautious when dealing with precision of 0.0001 inch and finer.

Good quality micrometers also have some provision for an adjustment to eliminate backlash resulting from wear in the screw thread and mating nut. Again, the technique differs from brand to brand and is described in the printed material that came with the tool. In truth, it takes a very long time indeed for detectable wear to develop.

After use, always clean off the exterior of a micrometer before storing it away, but do not use compressed air for this, as dirt may get forced into the concealed threads. If a micrometer feels sticky or notchy in action, do not continue to use it—there may be something trapped in the threads, and further use will only damage them. The tool will have to be dis-

mantled, a job perhaps best left to experts. Finally, do not store a micrometer with the spindle screwed down onto the anvil; for some reason that I, at least, do not understand, this seems to encourage corrosion of the contact faces.

The Dial Indicator

The dial indicator is the second most common precision measuring tool, after the micrometer, that a serious mechanic is likely to encounter . . .and to buy for himself. Yet dial indicators (and the related test indicators, below) do not really measure the actual size of anything! Unlike rules, slide calipers, or micrometers, they do not gauge a dimension directly; rather, they are *comparison* instruments—they indicate the amount by which a certain dimension varies from some reference. This should become clearer as we describe the nature and use of the device.

The instrument comprises a circular housing with a clock-like dial face and pointer, plus a plunger that extends out from the housing. The most common has the plunger protruding downward; these are termed "side plunger" (or sometimes "bottom plunger") designs.

In the alternative "back plunger" design, the plunger extends out from the back of the instrument. At the end of the plunger there is a No. 4-48 screw thread for the attachment of various interchangeable contact points having flat, round, or pointed shapes. The screw thread also allows the fitment of extension rods, to increase the "reach" of the instrument. Typically, these come in 1-, 2-, and 4-inch lengths, and since each has corresponding male and female threads at opposite ends, they can be stacked to give extensions in 1-inch increments from 1 to 7 inches.

Within the case, the plunger drives a rack that meshes with a gear, which in turn drives other gears, ultimately connected to the pointer. By this means, the linear movement of the plunger is amplified, and the distance it has traveled is thus indicated on the gauge face.

Both the face and the "guts" of a dial indicator resemble those of a clock. The instrument comes by this likeness honestly: The origins of the dial indicator can be traced to the Waltham Clock Co. of Waltham, Massachusetts, perhaps sometime in the 1930s. The dial indicator came into its own in World War II; it made possible the gauging of the precision gear teeth needed for high-speed rotating machinery.

As in much quality "clockwork," jeweled bearings are sometimes used in dial indicators, although this is a matter of dispute among various manufacturers. One eminently respectable maker promotes this as a significant feature; another equally reputable firm insists on the superiority of its own bronze bushed internal works.

Although there are "long-range" dial indicators with a plunger travel of as much as 12

In some situations, rigidity of the setup can be improved over a conventional magnetic base with special-purpose fixtures, such as this magnetic "deck bridge," used here for precisely measuring piston-to-deck clearance. The design and use of special fixtures like this are eased by a design convention for dial indicators that sets the stem diameter at a standard 3/8 inch. *Powerhouse Products*

In either case, it should be obvious that even with comparatively "coarse" resolution, crowding so many markings onto a face a couple of inches in diameter would render them completely unreadable. Accordingly, the instrument is conventionally arranged so that, over the full range of the plunger travel, the pointer makes a minimum of 2 1/3 revolutions. This convention is part of a set of specifications—the American Gage Design (AGD) standards—developed in 1945 by the U.S. National Bureau of Standards. AGD specifications also stipulate dial face sizes (approximately 1 3/4, 2 1/4, 2 3/4, and 3 1/2 inches in diameter, coded as Groups 1 through 4 respectively) and certain other aspects and dimensions of dial gauges, including standardizing the diameter of the plunger stem at 3/8 inch, plus a requirement that every instrument be accurate to at least ± one dial division.

Given the wide variety of dial face graduations, and given that instruments with more than, say, 0.125 inch of plunger travel may involve many more than the minimum two full revolutions (plus) of the pointer, there is obviously the potential for misinterpretation of the dial reading. Wholesale confusion is avoided by two features. First, the AGD specs wisely require that, whatever increment the individual *marks* on the dial face may indicate (0.0001 inch? 0.0005 inch? 0.001 inch?), every *number* on the dial expresses 0.001 inch. (For metric instruments, AGD specs call for every number on the dial to indicate 0.01 millimeter.) Second, if full plunger travel corresponds to more than the conventional two-and-a-bit revolutions of the pointer, then it is usual for manufacturers to offer a "revolution counter"—a second,

inches, and others with a total range of just 0.015 inch, the most popular general-purpose models typically have a range of either 0.125 or 0.250 inch. Likewise, dials may be graduated in units of 0.0001, 0.00025, 0.0005, 0.001, or 0.010 inch (there are even units with 0.00005-inch markings), but 0.0001- or 0.001-inch graduations are most common.

Whatever the size of the graduations, dials come in two basic types, "continuous reading" and "balanced." On a continuous reading dial, the numbers wrap around clockwise from 0 to the full scale reading, starting and ending at the "12 o'clock" position. These are usually found on long-range instruments. By contrast, a balanced dial has positive numbers on the right-hand side of the dial and negative numbers on the left-hand side so, for example, if a shaft that is eccentric by 0.002 inch is rotated slowly under the plunger foot, the pointer will swing back and forth between +0.001 and -0.001. This is the arrangement usually preferred by machinists who are often concerned with "plus-and-minus" tolerances (and is the scheme found almost universally on dial *test* indicators—see below). Mechanics, as opposed to machinists, may find the continuous reading face more useful in some circumstances.

The phasing of cam action relative to crank rotation can be gauged using a dial indicator, together with a degree wheel, to measure the motion of camshaft lifters, a process known as "degreeing" the cam. In this case, only the point of maximum travel need be identified, so even large errors in alignment are unimportant. If the actual dimension is to be accurately measured, the line of plunger travel has to be parallel to the line of lifter movement. *Doug Gore photo, courtesy* Open Wheel *magazine*

A side lifting lever conveniently allows retracting the plunger foot to clear obstacles, and permits lowering the plunger gently onto the object to be gauged. Side thrusts on the plunger, or allowing it to slam onto the work, do not improve a dial indicator's health. *Federal Products Co.*

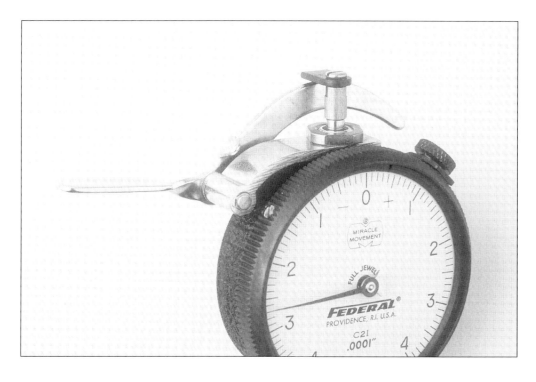

Dial indicators are *comparative* instruments. While the distance from the crank centerline to the block deck surface (the "deck height") may be of interest, of arguably greater importance is its uniformity from end to end and side to side. A fixed-length gauge bar allows a dial indicator to gauge this variation. *Powerhouse Products*

smaller rotary indicator inset into the main dial that tells the user which revolution the main pointer is on. If a dial gauge you decide to purchase offers this feature as an option, by all means go for it. Also, while inch reading dial gauges may have white, black, or red (or occasionally green) faces, metric ones are always yellow.

Note that AGD specs call for a minimum of 2 1/3 revolutions, not exactly 2 (and most manufacturers make it 2 1/2). Note also that the rest position of the pointer is at "9 o'clock." The extra part revolution and this offset in the pointer allow the instrument to be "preloaded," to take up any backlash in its internal gear train.

Use of the Dial Indicator

We have suggested that a dial indicator is not, by itself, an independent measuring tool; to be of any use, it must be combined with some other apparatus. In a machine shop or at a quality control inspector's station, it will most likely be used as a comparator—it will measure the dimensional difference between some reference object and the workpiece being measured.

In automotive mechanical work, the dial indicator needs, at least, something that holds it in place while some other type of comparative measurement is taken. An example of this might be the measurement of the end play of a crankshaft or camshaft in its bear-

ings. Here, the comparison is between one position of the shaft and another.

In such a situation, the indicator is most likely secured to a magnetic base, itself clinging to the engine block, though other types of bases are available. To connect the indicator to the base, the most usual arrangement involves a stout rod or "base post" projecting from the base, plus a crossbar that is secured to the base post by a swivel clamp, allowing the crossbar to be positioned at virtually any height and angle. For attachment to the crossbar, the instrument is usually built with a projecting lug on the back, with a 1/4-inch hole through it. Care should be taken to keep all the "overhangs" to a minimum, to eliminate as much spring in the setup as possible.

Bear in mind that the only thing a dial gauge actually measures is the movement of its own plunger. If the plunger is not exactly aligned with the work, an erroneous reading will be given. The situation is not as critical as you might think, however. First, recall that the accuracy of an AGD dial indicator is ± one dial division. Second, let's assume that the instrument is marked off in 1-thou increments, and that its total range is 0.125 inch. Even if the dimension being measured (or, more correctly, the difference between the positions being compared) is near the gauge's limiting range, the "cosine error," as it is called, that arises from a misalignment of 5 degrees—quite apparent to even an unskilled eye—will be just 4/10 of 1 percent of 0.125 inch, or less than half a thou. Clearly, straight by "eyeball" is generally quite good enough, except when something closer to 0.0001 inch accuracy is needed, in which case the parallelism between the plunger

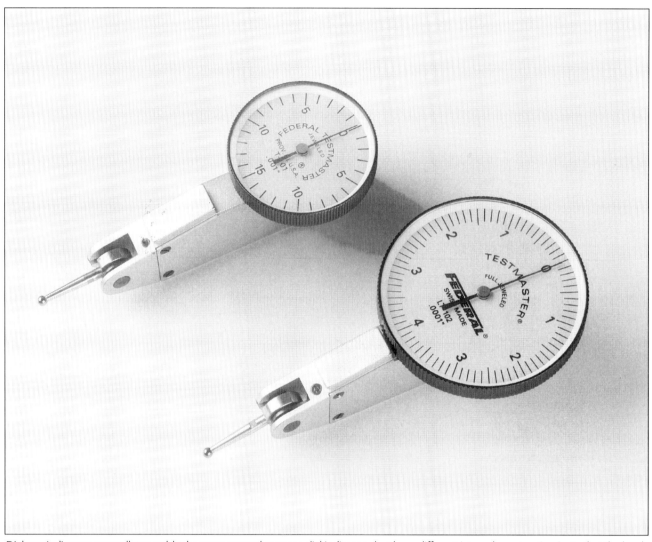

Dial test indicators generally resemble the more general-purpose dial indicators, but have different internal construction (note that the hard-tipped contact lever moves crosswise, not up-and-down), and are generally used in different applications. Their range is more limited than that of a dial indicator, but the instrument is generally more compact. Balanced dials are near universal. *Federal Products Co.*

and the work may need to be confirmed with a machinist's square.

Once the work is arranged in place, and with (in our example) the crank or camshaft pushed to one extreme of its end travel, the worker will typically preload the dial indicator about one quarter-turn, so the pointer is approximately at the "12 o'clock" position, then the instrument is zeroed. (It is not necessary to fiddle about endlessly with the setup, trying to get the pointer to line up exactly with the "zero" on the dial;

the dial face is attached to the surrounding movable bezel, and so can be turned.) When the shaft is pushed in the opposite direction, taking up the end play, the dial indicator will now display the total travel.

Some dial gauges come with a "shockproof" mechanism that greatly reduces the risk of damage from a sudden sharp impact, by allowing some internal components to disengage themselves momentarily if the foot moves too suddenly. Still, dial gauges are deli-

cate instruments (more so than micrometers) and while they do not need to be handled like fine china, their accuracy and life are not likely to be enhanced by ham fistedness.

Obviously, you should take care that it does not get dropped, and the contact foot on the plunger should not be allowed to slam against the work. On side-plunger (bottom plunger) indicators, the plunger extends through the diameter of the case, and the protruding stump can be grasped (once its protective cap

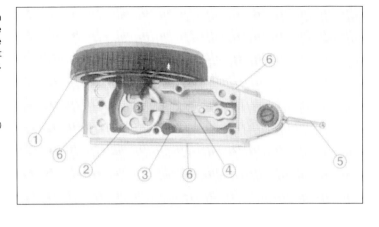

Similar to a plunger-like dial indicator, a test indicator uses a train of gears to amplify movement of the contact point. The sideways motion of the contact lever, however, means the input to this gear train comes from a sector gear arrangement rather than the rack and pinion of a plunger-type instrument. *Mitutoyo/MTI Corporation*

1. "O" ring incorporated in new bezel design seals instrument from dust and oil mist.
2. Enlarged pitch of teeth on crown gear improves ability of indicator to withstand shock.
3. Rubber bumpers limit travel of sector gear and prevent damage due to excessive travel.
4. Special alloy of sector gear provides greater resistance to wear, and longer distance between pivot points of linkage betters protection against shock.
5. Carbide point, .078" DIA., is standard.
6. Dovetails, integral with housing, give broad flexibility for mounting of instruments.

has been unscrewed) to manually raise the plunger and so control its descent onto the workpiece. A valuable accessory is a finger lift attachment extending to one side.

It also important to avoid driving the plunger hard up against its end stop. One way to prevent this, and to avoid imposing violent blows to the mechanism, is to arrange things so that the plunger moves *away* from the case during the measurement, rather than toward it. In the above example, it would be preferable to have the shaft pushed fully toward the gauge before the instrument is brought in contact, preloaded one full turn, and zeroed. Then tapping on the shaft would tend to unload the gauge.

In another situation, the dial gauge might be used to measure, say, the "runout" of a shaft. In this case, assuming the usual 2-plus turn instrument, the gauge would be loaded about 1 1/4 turns, leaving 1 full turn in either direction available for gauging "plus" and "minus" variations. The shaft should be rotated slowly; never attempt to use a mechanical dial indicator to measure any fluctuating value (valve lift, radial or axial runout of a pulley, etc.) on a running engine! The amplification of movement that takes place in the

instrument's internal gear train would destroy the tool. Besides, there is no earthly way you could read the wildly flailing pointer.

With the use of some very sophisticated (and expensive) circuitry, certain electronic instruments, such as some dial test indicators (see below), are able to accurately read rapidly varying values, such as occur when the runout of a circular part is being checked while the part is rotating at quite a high speed. But within our price range, any digital electronic instrument is likely to have internal circuitry that requires a little time to "decide" on the value being measured. If the value is constantly changing, as it is when visualizing and measuring runout in this way, the value doesn't stand still long enough for the instrument to do the calculation. The result would be either a blank stare from the gauge or a meaningless flickering of numbers. A mechanical gauge is often preferable to an electronic one for this sort of measurement of a value that changes, say, once per second.

Dial Test Indicators

To the uninitiated, a dial test indicator appears to be very much the same thing as a dial indicator, as described above. Indeed, there are

strong similarities and the distinction between the two seems, on the face of it, to be trivial, or at least arbitrary: While a dial indicator uses a rack-and-pinion mechanism to convert a linear movement into pointer rotation, a dial test indicator uses a lever and sector gear arrangement for the same basic purpose. Thus, while the plunger on a dial indicator moves in the plane of the dial face, the stem of a test indicator moves at right angles to that plane, in a slight arc.

This difference in construction proceeds out of the differing ways these instruments are used. A dial indicator, with its potentially longer range, is a versatile general-purpose instrument, but the fact that the plunger travels in a straight line toward or away from the gauge makes certain kinds of measurement awkward. By itself, it cannot be used to measure the circularity of an inside diameter being machined on a lathe, for example.

While a dial indicator can be adapted for this kind of measurement using a bell-crank accessory, a dial test indicator can be used directly, because its stem moves sideways rather than linearly. These instruments tend also to be more compact than their relatives, which further recommends them for such applications. They are often mounted onto a machine tool such as a lathe and used to measure even as the work is rotating at a good clip. Even for outside measurements, where a plunger-type instrument could be used, the shallow angle of contact between the stem tip (invariably carbide) and the work makes the test indicator much more able to cope with a moving workpiece.

Dial test indicators are also frequently attached to height gauges, as noted in Chapter 2, to improve the accuracy and convenience of those tools when they are used for comparative measurements.

Gauge Blocks

In previous chapters we have made occasional reference to gauge blocks—the most accurate standards of length available outside a laboratory setting. Although the cost of a full set of the most

accurate grade of blocks can run to near five figures, the price plummets if just a little less accuracy can be tolerated. A set of blocks of Federal Grade 2 accuracy (see below), can be had for about $1,000, with sets of lesser accuracy even more reasonably priced. For a shop engaged in high precision work on a regular basis, such an expense may be justified.

The most accurate (and most expensive) blocks are Federal Grade

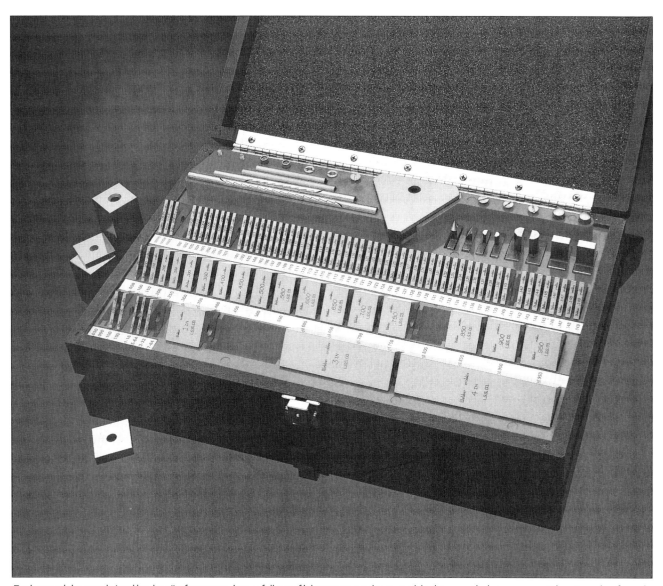

Far beyond the needs (and budget!) of most readers, a full set of laboratory grade gauge blocks nevertheless represent the pinnacle of purely mechanical measuring devices. They are accurate to within one-*millionth* of an inch—about 1/3,000th the thickness of a human hair! Smaller sets of lower grade blocks may be worth thinking about, however. *L.S. Starrett Company*

A test indicator has an advantage over a plunger-type dial indicator in situations in which a linear plunger would need a bell-crank linkage of some sort to "reach into" the work. The usually smaller overall size also helps. Here, the concentricity of the clutch housing and the crankshaft is being checked. *Doug Gore photo, courtesy* Open Wheel *magazine*

0.5, also termed "laboratory masters," which are certified to ± one-millionth of an inch over a 1-inch length, and Federal Grade 1, accurate to ± two-millionths. These are invariably kept under lock and key in an air-conditioned room and are used only to check other, "working" blocks, bearing designations Federal Grade 2 or 3, and which are certified to plus four-, minus two-millionths, and plus eight-, minus four-millionths, respectively.

The less expensive Grade 2 or 3 working blocks are commonly made from alloy steel, often SAE 52100, a high-carbon alloy steel frequently used for ball bearings. A material that is more resistant to wear and corrosion, such as tungsten carbide or chromium carbide, is usually used for Grades 1 and 0.5. These harder materials will retain accuracy longer in a shop environment, so are also often used for working grade blocks. More recently, gauge blocks made from ceramic material have been introduced; these lie between the steel and carbide materials in terms of cost and durability.

Although individual blocks in various sizes are available, most shops that have need of gauge blocks acquire them in sets. The selection of individual sizes of block that form a set has been worked out to permit stacking blocks together in various combinations to permit direct measurement over a useful range of lengths in very fine increments. For example, most if not all companies selling inch-sized gauge blocks offer a set of 81 blocks that can be assembled to produce total lengths of 0.100 inch to 12.000 inches in 0.001-inch steps, and from 0.200 inch to 12.000 inches in 0.0001-inch steps.

It might seem that stacking blocks together must necessarily reduce total accuracy. In fact, the extreme flatness and smoothness of the working faces allows "wringing" blocks together, leaving essentially no space whatsoever between them. The first time you are allowed to do this "wringing," it turns out to be an odd experience: After the working surfaces are cleaned free of any foreign matter (but not de-greased), the blocks are brought together flat and, using only moderate finger pressure, twisted (or "wrung") lightly together. Holy smoke! They stick together! Indeed, a tall stack consisting of a dozen individual blocks can be picked up by grasping the top one.

If this wringing is done correctly, the accuracy of the length of the assembled stack can potentially exceed the known level of accuracy of any individual block in the stack, a matter that has been confirmed many times in practice. What is surely happening is that the minuscule tolerances of the various blocks tend to cancel each other out.

While a large set of laboratory grade gauge blocks is far beyond the budget and the needs of most readers of this book, one or two working grade blocks of a suitable size can be mighty useful to have in a toolbox, to serve as a basic reference of known size to permit checking the accuracy of the remainder of one's precision measuring tools. Comparatively inexpensive sets of a smaller number of blocks are available, specifically for checking micrometers.

CONTENTS

Inside Calipers 47

Slide Calipers 48

Taper Gauges 49

Telescoping Gauges 49

Small-Hole Gauges 52

Thickness ("Feeler")
Gauges 52

Plastigage™ 54

Inside Micrometers 54

Bore Micrometers 57

Dial Bore Gauges 58

Depth Gauges 59

While not capable of micrometer precision, calipers are potentially more accurate than their simplicity might suggest. They are particularly useful for gauging the "truth" of a hole. With a light touch, variations of an inside diameter as small as a couple of thou can be detected. As with their outside gauging equivalents, there are versions with a transfer leg, to permit withdrawing the tool from awkward recesses. *L.S. Starrett Company*

MEASURING A GAP

In the previous two chapters we discussed measuring a span—the outside dimensions of objects. In this chapter we will deal with inside measurements or, as we have termed it, measuring a gap. In general, inside measurements are somewhat trickier than outside ones, partly because you often cannot really see what is going on, but also for some other reasons, as we shall soon explain.

While there are inside measuring tools for which there is no "outside" equivalent (feeler gauges are one obvious example), some of the tools used to measure a gap are simply "inside" versions of the same tools used to measure outside dimensions. Thus, there are inside versions of calipers, micrometers, etc.

Inside Calipers

As with their "outside" brethren, using inside calipers to measure a gap is a transfer measurement involving two steps: First the calipers are used to gauge the gap, often a round hole; then the spread between the points of the calipers is measured using some other measuring tool. Again as with outside

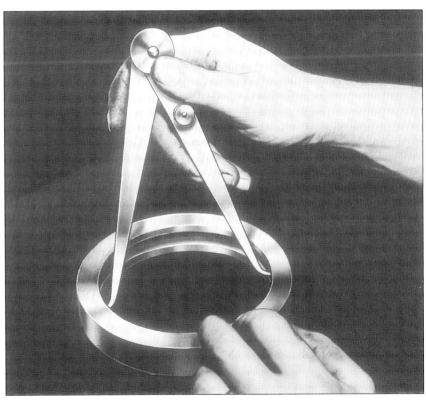

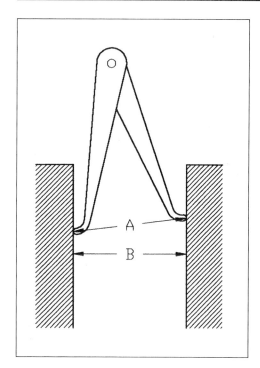
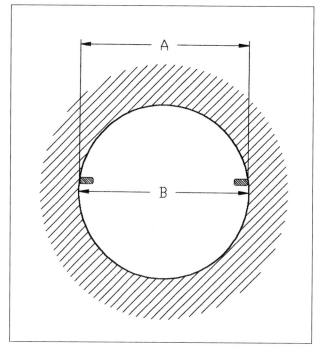

Inside measurements are more prone to error than external ones, in part because of the difficulty of being certain that the measuring tool is truly aligned with the dimension to be gauged. Any tilt of the tool (left) will lead to an exaggeration of the true dimension—dimension "A" is larger than dimension "B," the size of the gap. At the same time, failure to ensure that the tool lies along a true diameter (right) will lead to an underestimate.

calipers, properly handled inside calipers are capable of returning a result more accurate than the 0.01-inch divisions on a rule, and unlike outside calipers, gauging the setting of the calipers does not introduce any particular problems, so a micrometer might be used for this purpose. It must be emphasized, however, that the initial gauging is not likely to be accurate to any closer than 5 thou, and often not even that; in general terms, calipers are best regarded as accessories to a steel rule.

Apart from the fact that calipers are not really precision measuring tools, by our definition, there is the additional problem of determining that the tool is truly at right angles to the gap being gauged. Any slight amount of tilt will result in an error, always in the direction of exaggerating the dimension.

Also, when measuring a round hole, it is important to ensure that it is truly a diameter that is being gauged; if the tool is offset even slightly toward one side of the hole, an error that *under*estimates the true dimension will occur. Achieving decent results with calipers requires a very light touch, generally holding the instrument at the joint with just thumb and forefinger, patiently probing the gap until certain that the right dimension is being gauged. The correct technique is to use one leg as a fixed point and to rock the tool gently back and forth, gauging the drag of the other.

One place where this dirt-cheap, simple (indeed, almost primitive) device shines is in gauging the "truth" of a hole. A worker with a well-developed sense of feel can detect very slight amounts of

taper or ovality and, with experience, can estimate the variation in roundness to within a few thou. As with outside calipers, there are both friction and spring-bow types, and ones with a third transfer leg that allows one of the gauging legs to be retracted to clear obstructions outboard of the measuring point, such as when measuring the depth of a snap ring groove within a bore. As with outside calipers, 6- and 12-inch sizes are available.

Slide Calipers

The dial and Vernier calipers discussed in Chapter 2 are almost always configured to permit inside as well as outside measurements. About the only point worth adding here is that, while dial-equipped slide calipers can be read directly for both outside and inside measurements, on those with a Vernier

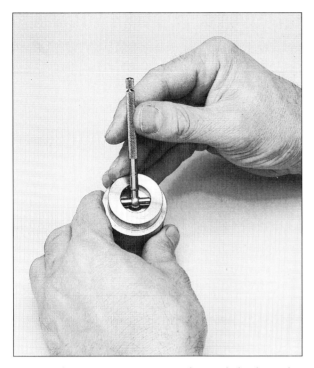

Once a telescoping gauge is entered into a hole, the tool is locked, then rocked about one of the contact points, using "feel" to ensure the true diameter is being gauged. *L.S. Starrett Company*

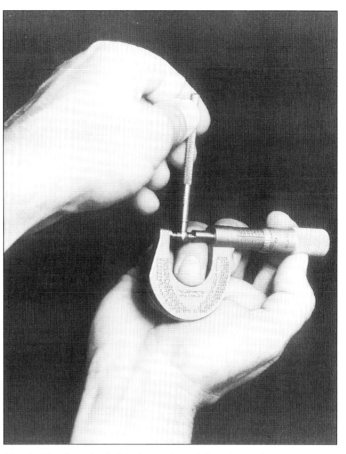

The locking function holds the setting of the telescoping gauge, so it can be withdrawn from the hole. The actual size of the hole is then gauged by measuring across the contacts using a micrometer. *L.S. Starrett Company*

scale account has to be taken of the width of the "nibs" used for inside measurements. This dimension has to be subtracted from the final reading to obtain the true dimension of the hole. (Note, too, that the width of the nibs sets a lower limit to the diameter of gap they can enter.)

Taper Gauges

The first thing to be said about taper gauges (also called taper rules) is that they do not measure tapers! The principle is dead simple: A thin, tapered piece of flat stock is pushed into a hole (or slot, or other gap) as far as it will go, and dimensions engraved on the tool indicate its width at that point. They do not allow "exploring" a hole for taper, but they are a quick and easy way to establish the diameter at the entry, and might even give an indication of any out-of-roundness at this point.

Two versions of this tool exist: Those that taper in width and those that taper in thickness. The first type may be graduated in either fractional or decimal inch units or in metric units. A set of four fractional inch rules measures from 1/16 to 2 1/16 inch in 1/64-inch increments; decimal inch taper rules come in sets of eight (0.100- to 0.500-inch) and 10 (0.500-inch to 1.000-inch), with 0.001-inch divisions. Equivalent metric reading versions, with 0.02-millimeter markings, span from 2 to 25 millimeters. The second, thickness tapering kind is calibrated in 0.001-inch increments on one face and 0.05-millimeter units on the other. The overall range of this tool is 0.010 to 0.150 inch/0.3 to 4.0 millimeters.

Telescoping Gauges

Inside calipers can be used to measure any gap that their legs will fit into, and because those legs are not hardened (and also because the tool is so inexpensive), they can be ground thinner to fit into really narrow cracks. Still, they are likely used most of the time to measure the inside diameter (i.d.) of holes. Another tool that can be used for

A telescoping gauge provides a controlled gauging force, while a handle protruding at right angles aids the user in aligning the gauge with the work. Both features enhance accuracy. Each gauge has rounded contacts having a radius less than the minimum size measurable, to avoid the end "bridging" over a curved surface. *L.S. Starrett Company*

exactly the same purpose is the telescoping gauge. Although its working ends are larger than those of an inside caliper, and so incapable of such inside measurements as the i.d. of a snap ring groove, the telescoping gauge is definitely preferable for gauging simple round holes because of its potentially greater level of accuracy.

That advantage comes from the construction of the tool: It amounts to two straight legs, one of which telescopes into the other, working against a spring that tends to extend it. Part of the improvement in accuracy over calipers is provided by that spring, which automatically controls the gauging force. Another aid to accuracy is a handle attached exactly at right angles to the fixed leg. The square alignment between the handle and the legs improves the mechanic's

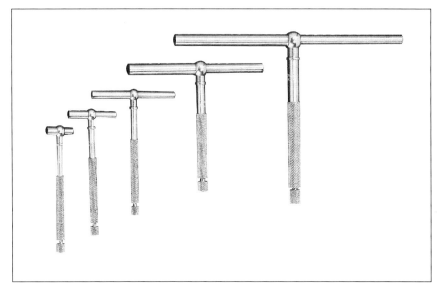

The minimum size of hole a telescoping gauge can measure is rather more than half the maximum size it can handle, because one leg has to fit within the other. Accordingly, measuring a range of spans requires a set. This group of five measures from 1/2 inch to 6 inches. *L.S. Starrett Company*

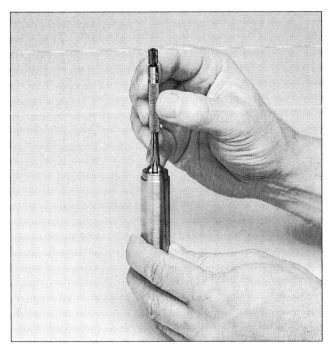

Small hole gauges based on the "split-ball" principle are used to measure holes below the lower limit of telescoping gauges. Turning the knurled knob at the end pulls on a tapered wedge that expands the ball. Once the user has confirmed by "feel" that the setting is correct, the span across the two halves of the ball is measured with a micrometer. *L.S. Starrett Company*

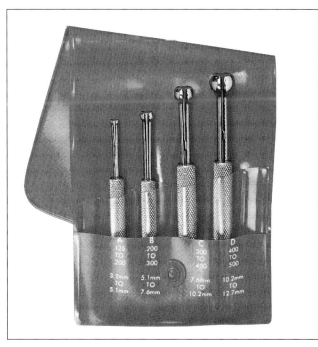

Limitations on how far the ball halves can be spread set a limit on the range of any single small hole gauge, so again a set is needed to cover a useful range of hole diameters. Telescoping gauges are usable above about 1/2 inch, so that is about as large as small hole gauges get. This set of four spans from 1/8 inch to 1/2 inch. "Half-ball" versions are offered for measuring very shallow holes and slots. *L.S. Starrett Company*

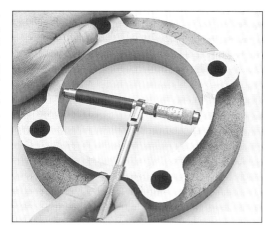

Inside "mikes" offer micrometer precision when measuring cylinders, rings, or the gap between parallel surfaces or caliper points. The range of a single tool having 1 inch of travel can be extended through the use of extension rods, as here. (Note the insulated handle on the extension rod.) A detachable handle aids in ensuring alignment of the tool in the hole. *L.S. Starrett Company*

ability to ensure that the tool is truly lying perpendicular across the hole. In a slightly more expensive version of the same thing, both legs telescope into a sleeve that supports them, the handle being attached to the sleeve. This feature means that the handle is self-centering, rather than being almost always offset somewhat toward one side of the hole, further assisting the worker in achieving a square alignment.

In use, the tool is gently manipulated in the hole until it seems to be measuring a true diameter, then a small knurled grip at the end of the handle is turned, which clamps the legs against movement. The tool is then gently rocked around, using one leg as a fixed point, probing the hole in much the same way as with inside calipers. Once satisfied that the gauging is true, the tool is withdrawn from the hole and the span across its contacts sized using a micrometer.

Because the amount of telescoping movement is restricted by the length of the legs, the range of any given size of instrument is limited. These tools are usually sold in sets of either four or six, spanning from 5/16 inch to 2 1/8 inch or 5/16 inch to 6 inches. The contact

ends of each size of gauge are ground to a spherical radius that ensures that the contacts do not bridge across the curvature of the smallest hole the tool can enter. The contact between the legs and the hole is thus concentrated at a point, rather than over an area or line, such as when a micrometer is being used to measure a rectangular or circular piece. The contact point of the gauge thus cannot help align the tool with the work. This aspect of telescoping gauges (and certain other inside measuring tools) is yet another reason why measuring a gap is somewhat more challenging than measuring a span.

Small-Hole Gauges

The smallest hole a telescoping gauge can measure is about 5/16 inch. Of course, there are great many holes encountered by mechanics that are much smaller than that. The small hole gauge is specifically designed for measuring holes, slots, and other gaps down to 1/8 inch. The actual gauging element is a ball, split across its diameter; the two halves can be spread apart by a tapered rod that is pulled between them by turning a knurled knob at the end of the handle the ball is attached to.

Limitations on the extent the split ball can be spread means that a set of four is needed to span the range from 1/8 inch to 1/2 inch. Once the correct size of tool is selected, the gauge is entered into the hole and the ball expanded by turning the knurled knob. (It is important not to overexpand the ball; if in doubt, just start "big" and keep working down until you find the first one that will go into the hole.) Once contact is obtained using standard gauging force on the knob, the handle is rocked slightly to ensure a true reading. The tool is then withdrawn and the diameter of the ball *directly across the split line* is measured with a micrometer.

As with telescoping gauges, the radius of the contacts has to be smaller than the smallest hole to be measured, to avoid bridging across the curvature. Thus, the contact area is again reduced to a point. However, because the ball is approximately spherical (and exactly so at some point in its range of expansion) and because the body of the tool is large in relation to the hole, gauging errors from slight misalignment of the tool in the hole are likely to be less than in the case of a telescoping gauge. Accordingly, if a hole you are trying to measure lies in the range of overlap between these two types of instrument (that is, between 5/16 and 1/2 inch), it would seem wiser to use the small hole gauge. Half-sphere gauges, completely flat on the bottom, are available for use in very shallow holes, slots, keyways, etc., but these are easier to misuse; the full ball type is preferable where space permits.

Thickness ("Feeler") Gauges

It should by now be apparent that, for most measuring tasks, there is more than one way to go about the job, and there are usually several different tools that might be used. When it comes to measuring gaps of less than about 1/8 inch, however, the choices are comparatively limited. In some cases, such as when measuring valve "lash" (clearance), a dial gauge or test indicator can be used to measure the difference between two positions of a part; in others, there may be no movement to measure—the end gap of a piston ring, for instance. In all such cases, feeler gauges may be used. Handled properly, they can yield an answer to at least 0.001-inch accuracy.

Thickness gauges (called "feeler" gauges by most everyone) are simply strips of tempered steel, about the length and profile of a finger (although extra long blades up to 12 inches are also available), that are precisely ground to a specific thickness, which is marked on the blade. They usually come in sets containing from a handful to dozens of individual blades, in either inch or metric sizes. Individual blades are made as thin as 0.0005 inch and as thick as 0.200 inch, but most sets sold for automotive work cover the range from about 0.002 inch to 0.020 or 0.030 inch. It is the way of the world that you will one day encounter a situation where the particular blade you need is missing or broken. Provided the surfaces of each blade are clean and undamaged, "stacking" two or more blades together to arrive at the desired total is completely acceptable.

Blades may be either straight or tapered, for reaching into narrow spaces; some have their ends bent at about a 45 degree angle, for the same purpose. Another variation is thickness gauges that use wire rather than flat stock. These usually have the wire bent into a narrow "L" or "U" shape, to permit entering into awkward spots; they are most commonly used to measure the gap between a pair of spark plug electrodes.

Obviously, a 0.015-inch blade simply will not go into a 0.010-inch gap, while a 0.005-inch one will slip right through. Judging whether that same gap is 0.008 or 0.012 is a bit trickier. It is difficult to describe the correct "drag" of a blade that tells you that you are right on. In general, the pull required to slide the feeler through the gap should be approximately standard gauging force—somewhere between 1 and 2 pounds, but it is really a matter of experience. Practicing using the known gap between the contacts of a micrometer is a good way to gain that critical sense of touch.

One common situation in which feeler gauges are used is in adjusting a clearance that has a tolerance. The clearance between a rocker tip and the end of the corresponding valve stem, for example, might be specified as 0.009–0.012 inch. A convenient and completely legitimate technique in such cases is to select *both* a 0.009-inch *and* a 0.012-inch blade, and use the pair as "GO" and "NO-GO" gauges—as long as the thin blade slips freely through the gap, but the fat one does not, you know the gap lies somewhere between the two.

A final point: Some mechanics use feelers to check the valve clearance on a running engine. These folks work fast, but their feelers, at least the ones most commonly used in this way, soon become covered with little dents. Extra thin blades are especially easy to damage in this way.

The minimum "closed" length of an inside micrometer with a travel of 1 inch is at least a couple of inches, but the principle can be applied to smaller holes if the travel is reduced to 1/2 or even 1/4 inch. This unit with 1/4 inch of spindle travel can enter a hole as small as 1 inch. *Mitutoyo/MTI Corporation*

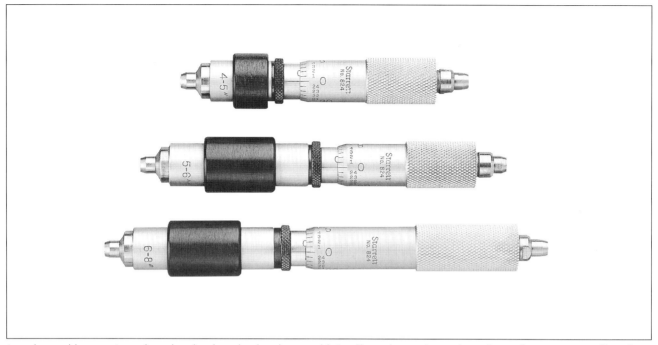

Interchangeable extension rods can be a hassle and, unless the assembly is calibrated every time rods are changed, accuracy can suffer. Where frequency of use justifies the expense, extension rods can be avoided by purchasing individual inside "mikes." Units are available to measure from 2 to 12 inches. In the larger sizes, tools with a 2-inch travel are sometimes encountered, such as the one at the bottom here. *L.S. Starrett Company*

Plastigage™

Then there are situations where even a feeler gauge won't fit. When measuring main bearing clearances, for example, the crank webs invariably get in the way. Here, you cannot even apply the indirect, "range-of-movement" technique, using a dial indicator, because even if there is any detectable movement, it may not accurately reflect the dimension you are trying to determine. (A crank supported in, say, three or five bearings will only move radially as far as allowed by the *tightest* pair of bearings; the others could be miles off.) Yes, you could dismantle everything and separately measure the outside diameter of each journal and the inside diameter of each bearing using an outside micrometer and a telescoping or bore gauge, respectively, but there is an ingenious alternative.

Plastigage™ consists of spaghetti-like strands of a soft plastic material, supplied in lengths of about a foot in a paper envelope with curious bar code-like markings on it. In use, a short piece (a bit less than the journal width) of the plastic strip is snapped off and set in place on the bearing surface, then the bearing cap installed and torqued to factory specs. (Note: The crank must not be turned at this point!) Once the cap is again removed, the plastic strip will be seen to have squashed flat, and its new width can be compared with the different stripes on the envelope. If the true clearance is anywhere near correct and the size of Plastigage™ originally selected is appropriate, its width when squashed will match up with one (or fall between two) of these markings. The number beside the matching stripe on

the envelope directly indicates the clearance, in "thou."

While it cannot tell you anything about out-of-roundness, and is dubiously useful as a measure of taper, Plastigage™ is a mighty handy way to establish overall average clearance of engine bearings. Many mechanics consider that it should always be used before buttoning up an engine after crank or bearing replacement as a quick final check. At least it will catch a set of mis-marked 0.020-inch undersize bearings on a 0.010 undersize crank, or vice versa, without the amusing noises that happen when this check is made by starting the engine!

Inside Micrometers

Everything we have discussed so far in this chapter as means of measuring a gap has, except for taper gauges and feeler gauges, involved a transfer measurement:

calipers, telescoping and small-hole gauges, and even "Plastigage," involve comparing the setting of a gauging device with a direct-reading measuring device of some sort. One means to directly measure the size of a hole or other gap is the inside micrometer.

The precision lapped screw-and-nut mechanism and the configuration of sleeve and thimble on this instrument are identical to that of a conventional external "mike," and the remarks made in the previous chapter regarding micrometers apply also to these instruments in almost every respect, with two exceptions. First, the markings on the sleeve and thimble are quite logically "backward"—the maximum value is shown when the spindle is fully extended (that is, in a big hole), and the minimum is shown when it is fully retracted. Second, the fact that the "back" end of the micrometer becomes a contact surface means that a

ratchet stop cannot be provided, although a friction thimble can be.

Because they are most often used to measure a circular bore, the contacts on both the body and the spindle are ground to a spherical shape. (In fact, some inside mikes are available with flat end contacts, for use when measuring rectangular gaps only. These are quite rare.) As noted in connection with telescoping gauges, this makes it difficult to judge whether the tool is "cocked" slightly in the bore, and the same "rock, lock, rock-again" checking has to be conducted if high accuracy is to be achieved. (A detachable handle that extends at right angles to the tool helps.) The limitation this places on accuracy is hinted at by the fact that inside mikes of this sort are all 0.001-inch reading. While the instrument may be mechanically accurate to more than 10 times that level of precision, it is essentially impossible to conduct the measurement with

sufficient accuracy to justify a Vernier "10th"-reading scale.

The irreducible length of the spindle-and-nut assembly (the micrometer "head") sets a lower limit to the size of hole or other gap that an inside micrometer can measure. With a micrometer head having the usual 1-inch range, the minimum hole size is typically 2 inches, although heads with a reduced range of 1/2 inch or even 1/4 inch allow the length of the body, and thus the minimum hole size, to be reduced to as little as 1 inch. In the same vein, while there are one-piece inside mikes up to 11 inches in length (that is, capable of measuring from 11 to 12 inches), by far the more common arrangement is to use a single head together with a number of precision extension end rods. Thus, a basic head with a range of 1 inch and a "closed" length of 2 inches can be fitted with end rods, offered in 1-inch increments, to measure

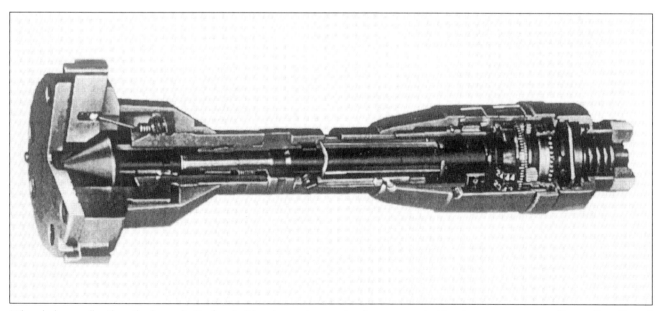

When holes smaller than the lower limit of an inside micrometer need to be measured with micrometer accuracy, "internal" or "bore" micrometers can be used. A micrometer head assembly is used to move a tapered plunger that spreads apart two or three contacts. Because the tapered plunger "de-amplifies" spindle movement, the range of any single instrument is extremely limited. *Brown & Sharpe, North Kingston, RI*

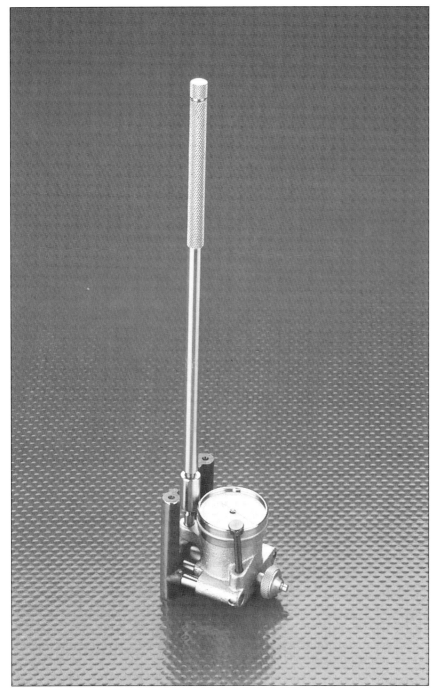

One form of bore gauge that is probably quite familiar is the "cylinder gauge"—essentially a dial indicator in a special-purpose housing. Being a comparison-type tool, it needs to be set with a ring-shaped standard or an outside micrometer, but can then be used to measure ovality or taper of any cylindrical bore. Apart from its use in cylinders, it is also often used to check the size and roundness of bearing bores. *L.S. Starrett Company*

Dial-type bore gauges are available for use in very small holes. Interchangeable probes allow one head to measure a range of sizes. Long versions are offered for use in deep holes. *Brown & Sharpe, North Kingston, RI*

up to 24 or even 32 inches. Shorter extension rods are often solid; longer ones are usually tubular, to reduce weight. (Although they are likely to be of limited use in automotive work, there are also larger-bodied instruments with a "closed" length of 6 inches, sometimes with a 2-inch working range, that can be fitted with end rods to measure to over 40 *feet!*)

Whether achieved by a micrometer with a large fixed body length or by the use of extension rods, and especially in the latter case, whenever the total dimension being measured is large, consideration has to be given to the problem of thermal expansion. Recall that steel expands by about 6.5 millionths per inch for every Fahrenheit degree rise in temperature. While this sort of variation is unimportant (indeed, almost immeasurable) over short spans, the effect begins to stack up as the total length increases. If, for example, a 12-inch extension rod starts out at a shop temperature of, say, 68 degrees and then, through heat transferred from the mechanic's hand, rises in temperature to, say, 81 degrees, it will have become longer by 0.001 inch! In view of

For hole sizes from about 1/8 inch to about 3/8 inch, one form of probe for a dial bore gauge uses a sliding shoe (the maker terms this a "centering-size disk"). *Brown & Sharpe, North Kingston, RI*

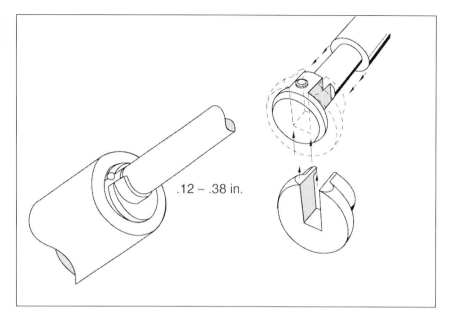

.12 – .38 in.

this, extension rods are often supplied with insulated grips. In any case, it is wise to avoid handling extension rods for any longer than necessary, and/or to use a shop rag or some other means to reduce transfer of body heat to the tool.

A distinction needs to be drawn here between the instrument just described (sometimes termed a "stick" micrometer), which essentially consists of just a micrometer head, and an inside *micrometer caliper*. This last has a pair of caliper-like gauging jaws extending out at right angles to the tool, one attached to the end of the spindle, the other to the micrometer head. (Obviously, the spindle does not rotate in this type of instrument.) The width of the jaws sets a lower limit—usually 0.200 inch—to the size of gap into which they can be entered. Apart from nominal "1-inch" tools measuring from 0.200 to 1.200 inches, other sizes are available from 1 to 2, 2 to 3, and 3 to 4 inches, all calibrated in 0.001-inch divisions.

Bore Micrometers

For direct measurement of hole diameters below the range of an inside micrometer, described above, a tool sometimes called an "internal micrometer" can be used. This comprises a cylindrical body having a conventional micrometer head at one end and, at the other end, a set of two or three contacts arranged radially around the spindle axis. Rotation of the micrometer thimble draws a tapered rod

between the contacts, causing them to expand outward.

The amplification achieved by the taper on the draw rod means that extremely high accuracy can be achieved with this instrument—most read directly in 0.0001-inch divisions—without the need for a Vernier scale. At the same time, that same magnification of the spindle movement means that the full range of travel of the tool corresponds to only a very small variation in hole diameter. Thus, an instrument that can measure holes down to 0.080 inch is limited, at the other end, to 0.100 inch. To span the range of 0.080 to 0.240 inch requires no fewer than five separate tools!

And the situation gets worse as the nominal size of the hole shrinks. In the case of one maker, instruments are available to gauge holes down to 0.040 inch, but to span the 40 thou from there to 0.080 requires another five! What is more, if this level of precision is needed, the accuracy of the measuring tool needs to be known with certainty, so precision master gauge

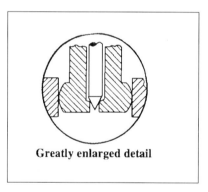

Greatly enlarged detail

For smaller holes, down to 0.037 inch, the type of probe used employs the split-ball principle, as seen on conventional small hole gauges. The familiar problem of small amounts of contact movement involving large amounts of plunger travel means that the range of any individual probe is severely limited, yet within that range 0.0001-inch accuracy is achievable. *Brown & Sharpe, North Kingston, RI*

rings should be used to confirm the zero point on the micrometer. Clearly, this is a very expensive way to go about measuring holes, but apart from having dozens of fixed gauges (simply lengths of precision ground round stock), there are few other ways to directly and very accurately establish the diameter of, say, carburetor jets.

Dial Bore Gauges

Another way to measure holes of a very wide range of sizes is by means of a dial indicator equipped with some additional apparatus. While not truly *direct* measuring—dial indicators, remember, are *comparative* measuring tools—when zeroed against an accurate standard they can return a result of microm-

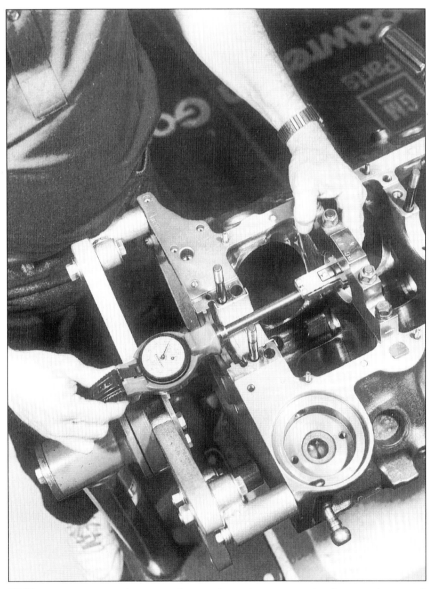

Dial bore gauges are perhaps most frequently used to measure the size, roundness, and taper of cylinder bores. They can also be used for the same purpose in main and rod bearing bores. Usually the bare bores are round within one or two tenths. Depending on the amount of bearing crush, the bore of the installed bearing shell can be distinctly oval with less clearance at the parting face than elsewhere. *Doug Gore photo, courtesy* Open Wheel *magazine*

eter accuracy. Such a combination of dial indicator and supporting apparatus appropriate for measuring a hole is termed a dial bore gauge (although in some cases they can also be used to measure rectangular gaps). They are among the tools most commonly used to determine the diameter, roundness, and straightness of engine cylinder bores, but comparable tools are available with much smaller ranges, for measuring small holes.

The additional equipment that permits a dial indicator to measure a hole is called a probe. It generally resembles the tapered-rod-and-movable-shoe arrangement used by bore micrometers. For very small holes, a variation on the split-ball principle described in connection with small hole gauges is employed. Yet another operating principle is a disk with a slotted hub that moves sideways relative to a fixed shoe.

Instruments operating on the split-ball principle from one manufacturer can gauge holes down to just 0.037 inch, and, from another maker, as large as 1.565 inch, all with a resolution of 0.0001 inch. The same range limitations that affect small hole micrometers (above) apply here, too, so while one maker offers a single tool with interchangeable probes to span from 0.0375 to 0.3940 inch, it requires no fewer than 24 probes to achieve this! Another manufacturer offers three split-ball units. One spans 0.107–0.266 inch, using five interchangeable probes; another 0.217–0.594 inch, using six probes; and a third for 0.560–1.565 inch, using eight probes.

For larger holes, say in the range of main bearing, connecting rod, and cylinder bores found in most automobile engines, the "movable-shoe" principle is most common. There may be either one or two fixed contacts, plus a movable one that is spring-loaded outward. The translation of the lateral movement of the shoe into a linear movement of the indicator plunger is usually achieved by a wedge that drives the plunger upward. A lever or trigger is often provided to retract the movable shoe when inserting the tool into a bore.

An arrangement of three contact points—two fixed and one movable—aids in centering the tool on the bore, *but does not guarantee it*; it is still important to rock the instrument slightly to ensure it is truly measuring a diameter. When just one fixed contact is provided, the problem of ensuring that the tool is properly centered in the bore is even more demanding, but this configuration is better able to detect out-of-roundness than the three contact arrangement.

Of course, once the size of the hole becomes large enough, a standard dial indicator, with its stem cap replaced with a suitable rounded contact point, can be entered crosswise into the hole. Given suitable extension rods for the plunger foot, the maximum bore size that can be measured is almost limitless. Note again, however, that it cannot measure directly; for such tasks, the indicator and a precision setting ring must be regarded as a "matched set."

Note, too, that while the indictors used in the purpose-made bore gauges discussed above are usually standard parts conforming to AGD specs, their dials are usually configured specifically for the range of measurement of the entire tool. To avoid potential (possibly expensive) confusion, it is not recommended that you attempt to economize by purchasing just the test probe(s), with the intent of attaching these to an AGD dial indicator you may already have on hand.

Depth Gauges

At its most basic, a depth gauge is just another variation on the rule. Intended for measuring the depth of holes, counterbores, etc., it consists of a rule—usually a narrow one, in view of its intended purpose—and a base through which the rule can slide, plus a means to clamp the rule in place. The base, which is machined flat and at right angles to the rule, is placed on a reference surface and the rule lowered into the hole or recess until it bottoms. After tightening the

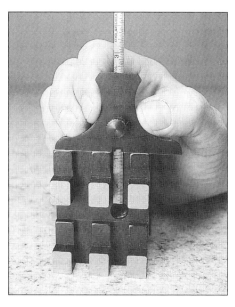

Conventional depth gauges amount to a rule that slides within a head. The head is set on the reference surface and the rule pushed down into the hole, slot, or other gap. A locking screw allows holding the setting, to permit the tool to be withdrawn for reading. Divisions are almost always fractional, typically not finer than 1/64 inch. *L.S. Starrett Company*

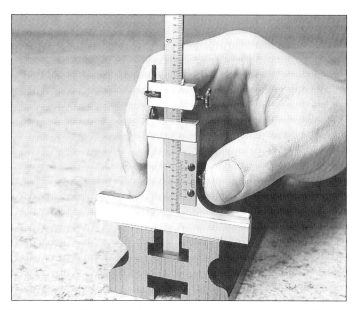

The Vernier principle can be applied to depth gauges, too, offering 0.001-inch precision on depth measurements. The same fine adjustment feature seen on other Vernier instruments allows more sensitive setting of the gauging force, and also helps reduce the tendency of the act of adjustment to lift the base off the reference surface. *L.S. Starrett Company*

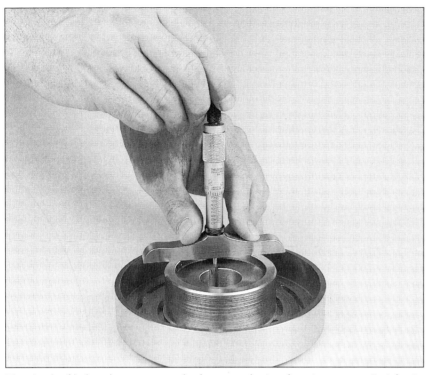

The depth of holes, slots, etc., can also be gauged using the micrometer principle. As with inside mikes, the engravings on the sleeve and thimble are "backward," so the tool reads zero with the spindle/plunger fully retracted. The inherent difficulties of making accurate depth measurements means 0.0001-inch accuracy is probably unattainable; these tools are invariably 0.001-inch reading only. (Of course, there are metric versions.) *L.S. Starrett Company*

When using a conventional dial caliper (or a Vernier caliper, for that matter) for gauging the depth of openings, accuracy is improved if the tool is given a larger base to rest on the reference surface. This simple clamp-on base is available as an accessory for such applications. *L.S. Starrett Company*

clamping nut, the tool is withdrawn and the reading taken. These simple, inexpensive tools are typically about 6 inches long, and are invariably graduated in 1/64 inch; accordingly, they fall well short of our working definition of a precision tool.

A rule with a sliding head is, in effect, a slide caliper minus the fixed jaw, and just as there are Vernier, dial, and digital electronic slide calipers, so there are depth gauges that incorporate these enhancements, making them precision tools. Most Vernier depth gauges incorporate a fine adjustment feature, and compared to a Vernier slide caliper rigged as a depth gauge, they have the advantage (in terms of accuracy) that the attachment of the base is fixed, rather than detachable.

Another type of dial depth gauge is simply a dial indicator secured to a beam-like base. (The terminology is ambiguous—a sliding graduated rule having a dial with a pointer driven directly by a rack and the dial indicator-based instrument we are discussing here are both called "dial depth gauges".) At rest, the contact point is usually recessed slightly within the base. To establish the zero point, the worker simply sets the base on a known flat surface, extends the plunger by pressing down on the stem until it makes contact with standard gauging force, and turns the bezel to zero the pointer. The base is then straddled over the hole and the plunger stem again pushed down with standard gauging force. Next the dial indicates the depth of the hole.

While dial depth gauges are sold as free-standing instruments, complete with base and extension rods, they are, as we have said, simply dial indicators, usually of

1-inch total range, packaged with these accessories. The bases are available separately and, since the AGD standards specify a stem diameter of 3/8 inch, anyone's base will fit anyone else's gauge.

Micrometer depth gauges are almost completely described by their name; they simply involve a micrometer head secured to a base. The one point that needs to be noted is that the graduations on the sleeve and thimble are "backward," like those of an inside micrometer. The standard inch-measuring tool measures from zero to 1 inch; interchangeable spindle extensions are available in 1-inch increments to permit measuring depths up to either 9 or 12 inches, according to the manufacturer. For holes very close to inside corners, where the base would prevent getting the tool over the hole, "half-base" versions are offered. While invaluable in certain situations, these exaggerate the difficulty of ensuring that the tool is firmly and squarely seated on the reference surface.

For most purposes, the depth of a hole can be gauged with nearly equal accuracy using a Vernier, dial, or micrometer depth gauge, and the choice among these alternatives is likely to be based on considerations other than accuracy. In this connection, it is notable that while a dial indicator calibrated in 0.0001-inch or even 0.00005-inch divisions could, in principle, be mounted in a base and used as a dial depth gauge, the indicators actually supplied in "prebundled" dial depth gauges are invariably calibrated in 1-thou

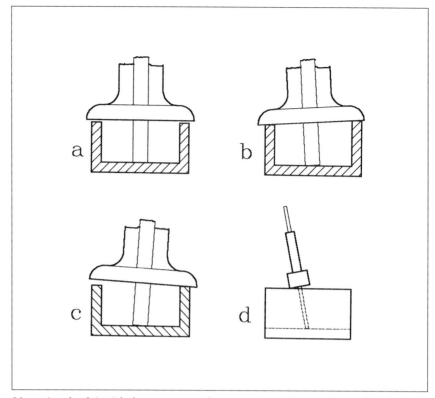

Measuring depth is tricky because so much can go wrong. The act of extending the gauging stem can cause the user to unwittingly raise the base off the reference surface (a); or the reference surface may not be level, as assumed (b); or the entire tool may be tilted side-to-side (c) or, even more likely because of the narrower base dimension, from front-to-back (d).

divisions. Equally notable, the micrometer heads that form the working parts of micrometer depth gauges are never equipped with a Vernier scale—they are 0.001-inch reading tools only.

There are a couple of matters to point out here. First, it is very rare that the depth of a hole is critical to within less than a few thou. (Indeed, it is uncommonly difficult to *produce* a hole with much greater precision.) Second, the above should give warning that depth gauges are notoriously difficult to

use with accuracy, whatever the level of precision of the basic tool itself. The main problem seems to be a tendency for the user to tilt the base slightly, especially across its narrow dimension, or to unwittingly raise the base off the reference surface when the extending probe is shoved down too firmly. (The automatically controlled gauging force of the dial instruments is a point in their favor here.) There is also sometimes a problem in being certain that the surface the base is resting on is truly flat and square.

CONTENTS

Angular Measurements . . 62

Straightedges, Parallels,
and the Machinist's
Square 63

Levels 65

The Angle Finder 67

Bevel Protractors 68

Timing Wheels/Degree
Wheels 69

The Sine Bar 71

Precision Angle Blocks . . . 71

Fixed Gauges 73

Gauging Threads 74

CHAPTER FIVE

MEASURING ANGLES, RADII, AND PITCHES

So far, we have dealt entirely with the use of tools for linear measurements—lengths or distances, expressed in inches or millimeters, and fractions of those units. In the remainder of this book we will mostly be considering the problems of measuring other kinds of quantities, the tools used to gauge them, and the correct use of those tools. In general, we will have to relax our standards for both precision and accuracy. While instruments for measuring linear dimensions with an accuracy of 1 part in 10,000 are fairly commonplace, most other physical quantities cannot be measured with anything like that level of precision, with a few exceptions. One of those exceptions is angular measurement.

Angular Measurements

In the inch system, linear measurements of less than a whole inch can be expressed as simple fractions, each one-half the size of the one before—1/2, 1/4, 1/8, and so on. This subdivision can obviously be carried on indefinitely, but a practical limit is reached at 1/64 inch, or sometimes 1/128. This is partly because at that point the markings on a rule become too closely spaced to read with the naked eye, and partly because until the standardization of the inch and the introduction of the micrometer, anything finer pretty much had to be achieved on the basis of hand fitting anyway.

The micrometer changed all that, yet for quite some time after its introduction, engineering dimensioning used a mixture of simple fractions (1/2, 1/4, etc.) and decimal ones (0.10, 0.010, etc.), and the shift to the near exclusive use of decimal fractions in the metal-working trades did not occur until the 1920s. The reason for this change seems mostly to be a simple matter of the convenience of calculation; it is generally easier to add, subtract, multiply, and divide when working with "tens," *because our number system is built that way.* (Of course, a system of multiples of tens, or tenths, is the very basis of the metric system.)

Now, there have been a great many different number systems over the ages that were based on numbers other than 10. While they may seem "unnatural" to us, some of them have their advantages. You can divide 12 up into halves or thirds or quarters, for instance; you can't do that with 10. One of the very earliest number systems was developed by the Sumerians, something like 5,000 years ago. Their "sexagesimal" system was based on 60.

And so we come to the reason circles are divided into 360 parts, rather than 100, or 1,000: The Sumerians divided the circle of the heavens into the 12 houses of the Zodiac, then further divided each "house." Since their number system was based on 60, there seem

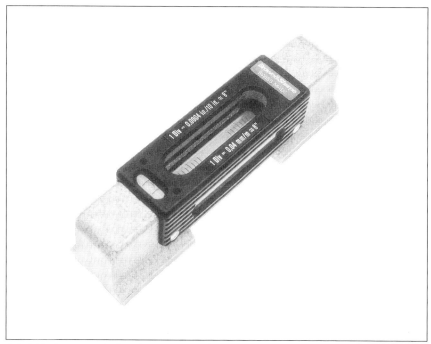

A bubble in a curved tube always rises to the *exact* top. The tightness of curvature of the tube or, as in the case of this precision engineer's level, the curvature of the barrel shape ground into the interior of a straight tube determines its *sensitivity*—how far the bubble moves for a given tilt of the base. *Brown & Sharpe, North Kingston, RI.*

depends on how far from the center you measure.)

Straightedges, Parallels, and the Machinist's Square

Surely the angle that most commonly needs gauging is 180 degrees—a straight line. The simplest way to check whether an edge is straight or if a surface is flat is to lay a straightedge against it. In many cases a machinist's rule may be adequate for this, but there are also precision straightedges expressly made for this purpose which are straight and flat within 0.00002–0.000050 inch, depending on make and grade. Coincidentally, 0.000050 inch is about the minimum gap you are likely to be able to see, even with optimum lighting.

If the situation prevents a line of sight, one alternative technique for gauging flatness is to prop a straightedge up on two equal thickness ("feeler") gauges, then to probe the resulting gap using a third identical feeler, or alternatively two of them, respectively 0.0005 inch thicker and thinner than the supporting shims. With an educated "touch," variations of a few "tenths" can be detected this way. (Recall that clean, undamaged feelers can be stacked; you do not necessarily have to buy three sets of gauges.)

Similar to the precision straightedge is a simple but precisely made rectangular block called a *parallel*. These come in matched pairs in sizes from 1/8x1x6 inches through 1-1/2x3x12 inches in either hardened steel or, in the larger sizes, granite. Limits on variation from straightness and flatness are the same as those for precision straightedges. These are widely used as spacers, shims, levelers, etc., both for gauging and inspection and in

grounds to speculate that the original unit of angular measure was thus 1/720 (12 X 60 = 720) of a circle, or 1/2 a degree . If this is correct, I can offer no explanation as to why that number got cut in half. Still, it is pretty clear that the base of 60 lies at the root of the matter. It was the Sumerians, too, who subdivided each basic unit—each degree—into 60 minutes, and each minute into 60 seconds. So do we.

Note, too, that in many branches of science and engineering (as distinct from technology, which uses engineering to build things), circles are divided up into *radians*. A radian is the distance that a radius of a circle "wraps" around its circumference. Thus, there are 2 pi radians in a circle. While the radian has some advantages for purposes of calculation, tools and instruments that measure angles are almost invariably gradu-

ated in degrees, minutes, and seconds, with one notable exception: Precision levels, discussed below, are usually graduated to give an indication of a slope expressed as fractional inches per foot (in/ft).

Since there are 60 seconds in each minute, 60 minutes in each degree, and 360 degrees in a circle, there are 1,296,000 seconds in a circle. Astonishingly, precision measuring tools are available that can measure angles with a resolution of 1 second and that have an accuracy as fine as 1/4 of a second . . .that is 1 part in 5,184,000! Thus, some angular measurements are capable of being conducted with precision and accuracy comparable to the most exacting linear measurement. (Of course, circles are not fixed dimensions, like inches or millimeters; they come in different sizes. How "big" 1 degree or 1 minute of arc is

While amateurs and low-buck teams make do with ordinary engineer's levels, well-funded teams can afford precision electronic version. These are required because as little as one-tenth of a degree of angle change on the front wing of an Indy car can vary the downforce (at speed) by several tens of pounds. *Doug Gore photo, courtesy* Open Wheel *magazine*

machine shop operations. When used as a reference to check flatness, the greater thickness of a parallel compared to the knife edge of a precision straightedge helps in one respect, because no extra set of hands is needed to hold the parallel on edge. On the other hand, that same thickness hampers gauging of the gap beneath it, whether by eyeball or using a feeler gauge.

The next most common angle encountered is the 90 degree (square) corner, whether inside or outside. The sliding square that forms part of a combination set is adequate for general work, but for greatest precision a fixed machinist's square is definitely preferable. These are far more accurate than

the usual sort of carpenter's square, the deviation from dead square between the thin blade and the thicker "heel" or beam being not more than 0.0003 inch over 6 inches, and in some cases as little as 0.0001 inch. Both flat and beveled edges are available, the beveled edge offering the same advantage of a visual line contact with the work as it does on a precision straightedge, but the thin edge is easily nicked.

Apart from avoiding dropping a precision square from bench height onto a concrete floor, and protecting it against rust, there are only a couple of other points worth mentioning concerning its use. First, when measuring an outside

corner (that is, using the *inside* of the intersection between beam and blade), be sure there is no accumulation of grime buried in this corner of the tool. Second, while a square may indicate that two surfaces are not at 90 degrees, it is often useful to know by *how much* they are out of square. A technique similar to that suggested for checking flatness with a straightedge may be used: If a tapered gap is observed, the size of the gap at its widest can be established pretty accurately with feeler gauges. That gives an answer in "thou-per-6-inches," and that ratio can be converted to an angle, if necessary, by a little trigonometry. (See sidebar, "Sine language.")

An "angle-finder," or *inclinometer*, is simply a weighted pointer that always aims straight down, in a housing marked in degrees. Among many other applications, it can be used to determine the inclinations of rear-end pinions, wings, drive shafts, or, as here, the steering knuckle. A magnetized case allows the tool to "stick" to any iron-based surface. *Doug Gore photo, courtesy* Open Wheel *magazine*

Levels

"Spirit" or "bubble" levels are perhaps most often thought of as carpenters' tools, but levels of various sorts have many potential applications in an automotive shop. For example, any kind of chassis setup work demands a level reference plane. Also, machine tools such as lathes do not take kindly to being bolted down to surfaces that are twisted, and one of the easiest ways to eliminate a diagonal twist over a few feet is by leveling across all four "corners."

It is meaningless to speak of the "accuracy" of a level, as such. A bubble trapped in a curved tube with the "bulge" facing up (which is how a carpenter's level works) will always rise to the *exact* top. With any slight inclination of the tube, the bubble will again find the exact top, although it will have moved along the tube somewhat from its original position. Just how far it moves depends on the degree of curvature of the tube, and it is this factor that determines the "sensitivity" of the instrument. In a tube curved to a large radius there will be more bubble movement per degree of tilt; with a tighter radius there will be less. Clearly, for a given length of tube, greater sensitivity means a smaller range, and vice versa.

Carpenters are generally satisfied if something is level or plumb within, say, 1/2 a degree, so the sensitivity of carpenter's levels (at least *my* carpenter's level—I just checked) is arranged so that about 1 degree of inclination will cause the bubble to move about 1/8 inch. The smallest tilt that is observable with that sort of sensitivity is about 1/4 of that, say 15 minutes (1/4

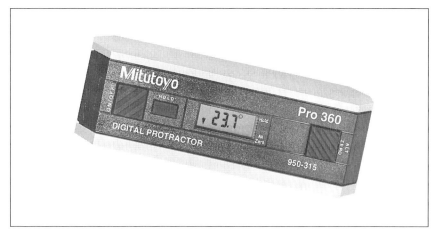

The resolution of simple, pendulum-type mechanical inclinometers is limited by size. An impractically huge scale would be needed to achieve the 0.1 degree resolution offered by this electronic version. In this case the manufacturer calls it a "digital protractor." *Mitutoyo/MTI Corporation*

degree). Now an inclination of 15 minutes corresponds to about 0.052 inch per foot (in/ft), which may not mean much when hanging a door, but when blueprinting an engine, even a 0.002 inch variation in the squareness between the cylinder block face and the crank centerline, for example, is considered sloppy. Over a block face length of, say, 2 feet, that still amounts to an angular error of no more than about 15 *seconds*—1/4 of a minute, or 1/240 degree. For a level to be a plausible alternative to precision linear measurement in such cases, much greater sensitivity is obviously needed than is offered by a carpenter's level. The engineer's precision level can provide it.

Instead of the curved glass or plastic bubble tube used in carpenter's levels, these precision tools employ a straight, ground bubble tube, or "vial." Now, obviously, a bubble in a straight tube full of fluid would be unstable; unless the tube was absolutely, perfectly horizontal, it would simply zip directly to one end of the tube or the other. To allow the bubble to respond to an inclination of the vial by moving

A precision bevel protractor is graduated directly in 1-degree increments, in four quadrants of 90 degrees each. A Vernier scale permits reading to 5 minutes of arc (1/12 of a degree). Accuracy is better than the finest possible reading. *L.S. Starrett Company*

off-center by a controlled and proportional amount, the vial is ground so that its i.d. is greatest at the middle and smallest at the ends, with a continuous, curving transition. (Pretty tricky job of grinding, if you ask me!)

Here the sensitivity depends on the contour of this ground inner surface. A gradual change in diameter will mean greater sensitivity; a more rapid variation in i.d. will reduce it. For a given sensitivity, the range of the instru-

ment will then depend on the length of the vial, and thus on the overall length of the tool. Precision engineer's/ machinist's levels are available with graduated markings on the vial face that indicate inclinations from about 80–90 seconds (corresponding to about 0.005 inch per foot) down to 10 seconds, or 0.0005 inch per foot. Such instruments are available in lengths from 6 inches to 20, the number of markings, and thus the total range of the instrument, varying accordingly. The flat bases on these tools usually have a V-groove down the center, to allow them to also be used on circular work.

It is both surprising and fascinating (to me, at least!) to realize that a tool as utterly simple as a level can allow inspection of the squareness of a cylinder block face relative to the crank axis, or to confirm that two banks of cylinders are at 90 degrees to each other, with a precision usually only achieved using very precise linear measurements. Of course, one reference axis—say the crank centerline—first needs to be jigged perfectly horizontal, and an accessory in the form of a fixed angle block with precise 45 degrees between its faces is needed. Still . . .

When using a level, it is considered good practice to use one that is no longer than the surface it is resting on; large amounts of overhang should be avoided. Also, recall that 68 degrees Fahrenheit is regarded as the "standard" temperature for gauging, so levels are calibrated for use at that temperature. The liquid surrounding the bubble is sensitive to temperature, expanding at higher temperatures and squeezing the bubble smaller; lower temperatures make the bubble larger. So, to avoid reading errors arising from changes in the length of the bubble, be sure to look at both ends of the bubble.

Finally, to check the accuracy of any level, simply set it on a known flat surface (the surface need not be absolutely level), and note the position of the bubble. Then turn the tool around and check again. Whatever the displacement of the bubble from center, as long as it winds up in the same relative position both ways, the tool is OK. Because the bubble cannot be in the "wrong" place, any discrepancy here implies that the base is not perfectly parallel with the vial; precision levels have some means of adjusting this. (Note that the adjustment should be *half* the variance.)

The Angle Finder

Another method for determining an angle with respect to the horizon is an *inclinometer*, also called an "angle finder." It consists simply of a weighted pointer and a dial marked in degrees, both housed in a case with at least two flat edges and one square corner. With one of the reference edges of the tool set against a surface, the pointer, always aimed straight down toward the earth, will indicate on the dial the number of degrees variation from horizontal or vertical.

Among a wide variety of other uses, such instruments are routinely used in race car "setups" to measure pinion angle, wing angle, and other

variables. A magnetized case is a convenience that allows the tool to "stick" to any iron-based surface.

Bevel Protractors

Measuring angles directly (as opposed to measuring the angle between a surface and a true horizon) is the function of protractors. At their simplest, these amount to a semicircular steel plate, graduated in degrees, with a swiveling arm and pointer that indicates the angle between the flat edge of the tool and the edge of the pointer arm. Although simple protractors like this are sold as free-standing tools, the protractor head on a combination square (see Chapter 2) performs exactly the same function, and has

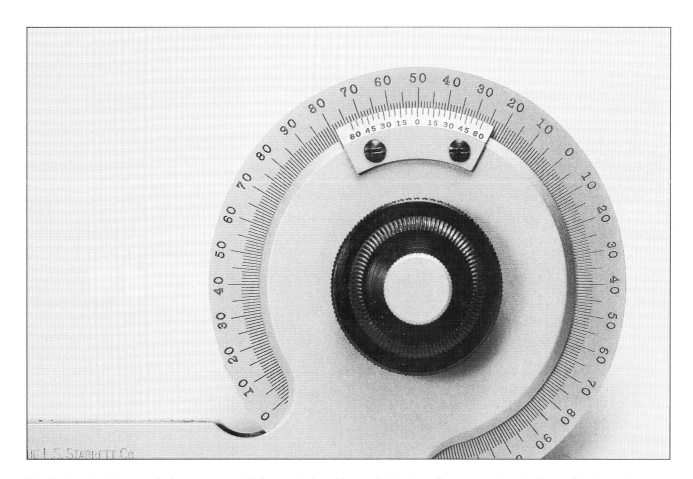

The Vernier principle as applied to a protractor. Each numerical marking on the Vernier scale corresponds to 5 minutes of arc. Here, the measured angle lies between 50 and 51 degrees, as indicated by the zero on the Vernier scale. Reading to the left (because the additional fractional degree lies to that side), the fourth line on the Vernier plate, corresponding to 20 minutes of arc, lines up with a line on the main scale. The final reading, then, is 50 degrees plus 20 minutes. *L.S. Starrett Company*

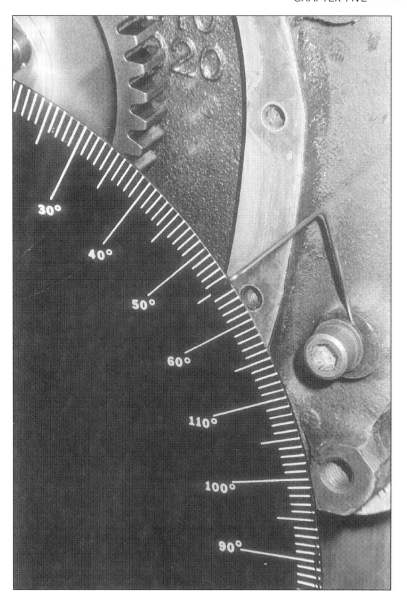

the advantage of incorporating a bubble level in the body of the tool. Here, the rule that forms part of the set serves as the pointer arm. Bearing in mind our cautions about "reading between the lines," both these tools can be reliably read to half a graduation, that is, 1/2 a degree.

When greater precision than that is needed, the Vernier principle is again used. Vernier protractors typically have a resolution of 5 minutes, with an accuracy somewhat better than can be read. Some have a fine adjustment feature for precise setting.

Timing Wheels/Degree Wheels

(See also timing lights, in Chapter 7.) A timing or "degree" wheel is nothing more than a protractor with a hub configured for attachment to the nose of an engine's crankshaft. In principle, one cylinder (usually No. 1) is set exactly at top-dead-center (TDC), and the wheel, loosely attached, is turned until the zero mark lines up

Used to establish valve and ignition timing, a "degree wheel" is just a circular plate graduated in degrees. Because it can be attached to the crankshaft in any attitude, zero can be wherever it is convenient to mount a fixed pointer. Fiddly final adjustments can be reduced by moving the pointer (here simply by bending it), rather than the wheel. *Doug Gore photo, courtesy* Open Wheel *magazine*

Establishing TDC (top-dead-center) on an assembled engine can be difficult. The task is eased by the technique described in the text, but an additional piece of equipment is needed—a piston stop. They are inexpensive to buy, but you can make your own for even less from an old spark plug, plus two nuts and a bolt with its end rounded. *Doug Gore photo, courtesy* Open Wheel *magazine*

with a pointer secured to any convenient surface of the engine. Then the timing wheel is snugged down. (For fine adjustment of the zero position, it is sometimes easier to move the pointer slightly than to fiddle endlessly with the wheel.) If the engine is now turned by hand, the phasing of various engine events such as ignition timing or valve opening and closing can be checked.

In practice, it turns out to be difficult to establish when a piston is at TDC. At the top (and bottom) of the stroke, the motion of the connecting rod big end is mostly sideways, so the movement of the piston over the few degrees of crank rotation either side of TDC can be difficult to detect. (The small amount of clearance around both the crankpin and the piston pin also confuses things.)

If the heads are off, a dial indicator can be used, but be sure to rotate the engine only in the normal direction of travel; rocking the engine back and forth around

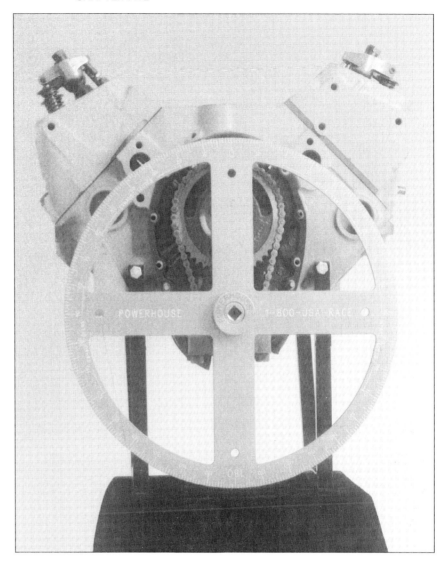

Really large diameter degree wheels spread out the individual degree markings, making for easier reading and thus higher potential precision. With large areas cut out of the center, they also allow the camshaft drive sprocket to be accessed without disturbing the position of the wheel relative to the crank. *Powerhouse Products*

Degree wheels are service tools; they must be removed before an engine is run. However, some aftermarket front pulleys and crank dampers, although smaller, have degree markings either around all of their circumference or, as here, over the range needed for ignition timing, at least. *Vibratech Division, IDEX Corp.*

You can always mark up your own front pulley or vibration damper. While it would be impractical to attempt to provide markings around a full 360 degrees, specific reference points, e.g, TDC plus the point of full ignition advance, are indicated. *Karl Fredrickson photo, courtesy* Stock Car Racing *magazine*

TDC will still reveal a "dead zone" because of the bearing clearances.

If the heads are in place, one additional piece of equipment is needed—a piston stop. (These can be bought at nominal cost, or you can make your own out of a junk spark plug, a 1/2-inch bolt with its point rounded off, and two jam nuts.) The stop is screwed into the spark plug hole and the engine turned (carefully) by hand in the normal direction of rotation, until the piston just contacts the stop. Beware of excessive force here, to avoid damaging the piston.

The degree wheel is then turned (or the pointer moved or bent) until it indicates zero. Then

the engine is turned *backward* almost one complete turn until the piston again contacts the stop. The wheel will now indicate some small number, say, 10 or 20 degrees. The wheel (or pointer) is them moved (toward the zero mark) exactly half of the original reading. Next, secure the wheel in place.

Although all commercial degree wheels we know of are marked in whole degrees, larger diameter wheels make readings easier and more accurate. Some really huge ones (16 inches or so in outside diameter), with most of the center area removed, have the advantage that the camshaft is accessible through the open space.

While many crank pulleys and vibration dampers are available with degree markings around the usual range of ignition timing advance, others are engraved around their full circumference. While their rather small diameter makes fine reading difficult, these can obviously serve duty as a degree wheel, but before counting on the results, be sure that the zero mark truly corresponds to TDC. Any slight mis-registration of the keyway in the crank or the damper /pulley will throw off all subsequent readings. Finally, stick-on tapes, marked in degrees, are available for certain standard damper diameters.

The Sine Bar

The extreme precision achieved by the most sensitive levels only applies to angles relative to a true horizon; when *directly* measuring angles, the best a Vernier protractor can do is a bit better than 5 minutes . . .about 0.018 inch per foot (in/ft). One way to directly measure angles with much greater precision than that is by use of a sine bar.

While the offerings of various manufacturers differ slightly, a sine bar consists basically of a precisely machined rectangular slab of tool steel, plus two equally precise steel rods. The rods may rest in deep V-grooves machined near each end of one face of the bar, or else may be inserted into holes, one near each end of the bar.

With the workpiece resting on a flat reference surface (often a surface plate), the bar is held against whatever angled surface of the workpiece is being measured. The difference in height above the surface plate of the two rods can then be gauged using a height gauge or other linear measuring tool. The angle formed with the reference surface can then be calculated, based on the measured height difference and the spacing between the V-grooves, which is usually either 5 or 10 inches, to at least 0.0001-inch accuracy.

As well as being used to measure an existing angle, a sine bar can also be used to set up an angle, to allow that angle to be machined on a part. In this case, one of the rods is rested on the reference surface and the other rod is propped up to some calculated height with a stack of gauge blocks.

Measuring angles using a combination of sine bar and gauge blocks has some drawbacks. Apart from the requirement for a set of gauge blocks, and the need to per-

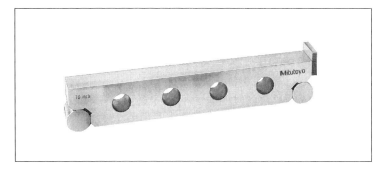

While awkward to use and requiring, in addition, both a set of gauge blocks and some head-scratching math, sine bars were the most accurate means to precisely measure and lay out angles until the comparatively recent introduction of precision angle blocks. *Mitutoyo/MTI Corporation.*

form some rather finicky mathematics, it turns out that the desired angle can only ever be approximated. Gauge blocks can be assembled to produce a stack of any height within the total range of the set in increments, typically, of 0.001 inch or 0.0001 inch. That fixed difference between one possible stack and the next higher (or lower) introduces an uncertainty that can never be eliminated.

Precision Angle Blocks

When angles have to be measured with extreme precision and accuracy, an alternative to sine bar methods is the use of angle gauge blocks. The principle is analogous to that of conventional gauge blocks: Highly finished pieces of hardened tool steel, or tungsten or chromium carbide, that can be wrung and stacked together. In this case, however, the blocks are tapered.

Because they can be stacked with either their "fat" and "thin" ends together or the other way around, blocks from a set of just six can be combined to produce any angle between zero and 99 degrees in 1-degree increments. A set of 11 permits measuring the same angular range in 1-minute steps; a

set of 16 offers increments of just 1 second.

As with conventional gauge blocks, several grades are offered. Working grades have an accuracy of 1 second; intermediate, "inspection" grades have an accuracy of 1/2 second; the very best lab master grades are accurate to within 1/4 second . . . one part in 5,184,000! The care, handling, and use of angle gauge blocks is the same as their square and rectangular counterparts; the higher accuracy grades should only be used to check working blocks.

Fixed Gauges

Sometimes the angular relationship between surfaces is critical, which is why precision angular measurement tools like those above were developed. Sometimes, though, the requirements are less rigorous. It does not matter much, for example, if the chamfer at the entry to a threaded hole is at the exact 45 degrees called for in a specification, or at 44 degrees or 46.

A simple and inexpensive tool that allows a check of such less-than-absolutely-critical angles is a flat template with two edges ground to a point of some fixed angle. When laid against the sur-

Sine Language: The Mathematics of Angles

Trigonometry is the branch of mathematics that deals with angles. In high school, it is often used to answer problems like: "A ladder needs to stand 1 foot out from a wall for each 4 feet up. How long a ladder do you need to reach to the top of a 10-foot wall? (So, math teachers have never heard of extension ladders?)

While a complete course in "trig" is beyond the scope of this book, the principles of its application are easy enough to grasp. Essentially, if the length of any two sides and the size of any one angle of a triangle are known, or if any two angles and one side are known, the "missing" angle(s) or side(s) can be calculated. For right-angled triangles, it is even simpler . . . only one angle and one side, or two sides need to be known to determine the remainder.

The "trick" to "trig" is a set of mathematical terms that refer to the relationships between the sides and angles of a triangle. There are six of them in all, but you really only need four. Those four terms are sine (abbreviated to sin, but still pronounced sine, like "sign"), cosine (cos), tangent (tan), and cotangent (cot).

It is not necessary to know what these mean in order to use them; the actual values of these for any angle can be looked up in a set of "trig" tables found in almost any high school math text or engineering handbook. And, working backward, once you have calculated the value of whichever of these trigonometric relationships you need (see tables below), then you can look up the corresponding angle.

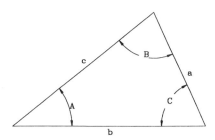

Figure 1.

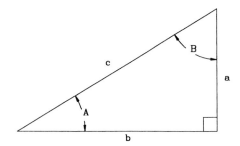

Figure 2.

For Oblique-Angled Triangles (Figure 1):

Parts given	Parts to be found	Formula
a, b, c	A	$\cos A = \dfrac{b^2 + c^2 - a^2}{2bc}$
a, b, A	B	$\sin B = \dfrac{b \times \sin A}{a}$
a, b, A	C	$C = 180 \text{ degrees} - (A+B)$
a, A, B	b	$b = \dfrac{a \times \sin B}{\sin A}$
a, A, B	c	$c = \dfrac{a \sin (A+B)}{\sin A}$
a, b, C	B	$B = 180 \text{ degrees} - (A+C)$

For Right-Angled Triangles (Figure 2)

Parts given	Parts to be found	Formula
a, c	A	$\sin A = a/c$
a, c	B	$\cos B = a/c$
a, c	b	$b = \sqrt{c^2 - a^2}$
a, b	A	$\tan A = a/b$
a, b	B	$\cot B = a/b$
a, b	c	$c = \sqrt{a^2 + b^2}$
c, b	A	$\cos A = b/c$
c, b	B	$\sin B = b/c$
c, b	a	$a = \sqrt{c^2 - b^2}$
A, a	B	$B = 90 \text{ degrees} - A$
A, a	b	$b = a \times \cot A$
A, a	c	$c = a/\sin A$
A, b	B	$B = 90 \text{ degrees} - A$
A, b	a	$a = b \times \tan A$
A, b	c	$c = b/\cos A$
A, c	B	$B = 90 \text{ degrees} - A$
A, c	a	$a = c \times \sin A$
A, c	b	$b = c \times \cos A$

face of the object to be measured, the fit between the part and the template—called an angle gauge—can be checked by eye. Although the angle templates themselves are devices of reasonably high precision (one maker lists an accuracy of plus-or-minus 5 minutes), the blades are quite short (perhaps 4 inches long), so the accuracy of gauging is more a function of the quality of observation than of the precision of the tool.

This arrangement, of course, only permits the measurement of inside angles although, depending on the geometry of the part, it may be possible to lay a straightedge along one surface of the part and to use the angle gauge to check the internal angle formed between the straightedge and another surface of the part. Greater flexibility and convenience for the measurement of external angles are offered by similar gauges that have notches as well as points.

These tools are available individually or in sets for angles from 1 degree to 10 degrees in 1-degree increments, 10, 12, and 14 degrees "by twos," and from 15 to 90 degrees "by fives." Related items are a gauge specifically for checking the 59-degree angle on drill points and a center gauge for checking the 60-degree internal and external angles on lathe centers and center drills, respectively.

Similar template-type fixed gauges with both convex and concave arcs ground into their edges can be used to check or lay out various radii. Such radius gauges are available individually or in sets, nested together in a steel frame, like a set of feeler gauges. The individual gauges, having all edges free, allow contact with a wider range of inside and outside fillets and blending curves. They are available in inch—both fractional and decimal—and metric sizes, from

Angle gauge blocks are to angular measurement what conventional gauge blocks are to linear measurement. Blocks can be "wrung" together with either their "fat" and "thin" ends together, or the other way around. A set of just six can thus be stacked to form any angle between 0 and 99 degrees in steps of 1 degree. Eleven blocks provide 1-minute increments; steps of 1 second (1/1,296,000 of a circle!) take 16 blocks. *L.S. Starrett Company*

0.010-inch to about 1-inch radius. A holder with a knurled grip, like that used to hold short rules (see Chapter 2), facilitates the use of these "loose" gauges in tight quarters.

Finally among fixed gauges are screw pitch gauges, sometimes called thread gauges. These almost always come in sets. At a glance, each gauge looks like a short section of saw. The teeth of the "saw" are ground at an angle and spacing to permit checking Unified National threads from 2 1/4 to 84 threads per inch (tpi) and metric threads with pitches from 0.25 millimeter to 11.5 millimeters. The blade on each gauge for the finer

pitches is greatly reduced in depth, to permit entering the tool into small diameter internally threaded holes. When used in combination with a caliper or micrometer (for gauging the outside diameter of externally threaded parts), or with a small hole gauge (likewise for internal threads), these simple gauges allow sure identification of the nominal size of almost any threaded component.

Gauging Threads

Obtaining accurate, detailed measurements of screw threads is a fussy, time-consuming business which, thankfully, is only seldom

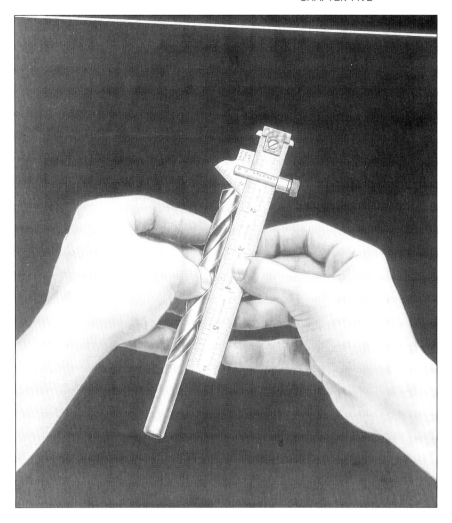

Fixed gauges for measuring angles are available in sets or individually. One special-purpose variation is for checking the angle at the point of a twist drill. *L.S. Starrett Company*

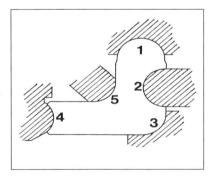

Fixed gauges can be used to check the radius of fillets and other curved surfaces. For each specific radius, a single gauge has five gauging surfaces to contact both inside and outside curves. *Brown & Sharpe, North Kingston, RI*

needed by most mechanics or machinists. Usually the main reason to measure any aspect of a threaded component is to sort things out when parts get intermixed by accident. This much can be achieved by a quick check on major (outside) diameter with a dial caliper or micrometer and with a fixed thread pitch gauge, as described above. Alternatively, a known reference part can be used as a fixed gauge. Thus, a nut with a known internal thread can be used to check the threads on a bolt or screw, and vice versa. Still, Murphy

insists that there will be times when things go wrong so, in the interests of completeness, here are a few tools and methods for performing more detailed measurements. We will start with internal (female) threads, if only because the gauging is simpler than the measuring of external (male) threads.

Unless they are very large (more than 1 inch in i.d.), about the only way to gauge internal (female) threads is with a single-purpose plug gauge—a piece of tool steel rod stock with precisely made threads on either end. The threads on the "GO" end should screw all the way into the hole with standard gauging force; the "NO-GO" end should start in the hole but, again using standard gauging force, should refuse to enter further than two or three turns. If the internal threads are too "small" in some respect, the "GO" gauge will not enter fully with normal gauging force. Thus, failure to accept the "GO" gauge is grounds for rejection too.

A plug thread gauge is very much a single-purpose tool. It will gauge only threads of one specific diameter, pitch, and class. To explain this last, the fit of threads is defined by a series of classes. Class 1 is a thoroughly sloppy business and has no place in any precision machinery. Class 2 is the most common found on automobiles and on general-purpose bolts and screws; it provides a modest clearance between mating threads, to reduce the chance of galling when parts are run together at high speed, as during production line assembly. Class 3 is the tightest, most exact fit that still ensures complete interchangeability; it is used universally for high-strength fasteners and other precision parts. There is also Class 5, an interference fit used when a manufacturer wants to ensure that a stud, for example, will not unscrew from a tapped hole when the nut on the other end is removed.

Plug-type thread gauges will reject a thread that is out of spec with respect to pitch diameter, major diameter, minor diameter, taper, or pitch, but it is not possible to say which of these variables causes it to "NO-GO." And once worn, the gauge becomes a paperweight; there is no adjustment, nothing to be done except get another.

Just as in the case of internal threads, fixed gauges can be used to check all the critical dimensions of an external thread at the same time. (A fixed gauge for checking external threads is an internally threaded ring—a glorified nut, if you will.) But also, as when gauging internal threads, it will be impossible to know just why the part passes the "GO" gauge but fails the "NO-GO" or, if oversize, refuses to accept the "GO" gauge. Ring gauges are seldom encountered in automotive shops, whether of a professional or a hobbyist/enthusiast. Besides, the fact that the threads on a male threaded part are external, and so visible and amenable to measurement, means that we can get much more information about them than a fixed gauge will reveal, and more than is the case with internal threads. (Incidentally, while seldom practical, it is possible to gauge an internal thread by making a plaster cast of it, then measuring the cast using the methods for an external thread.)

After a visual inspection for seams, surface roughness, bruises, etc., the critical dimensions of an external thread to be checked are the major and minor diameters, the

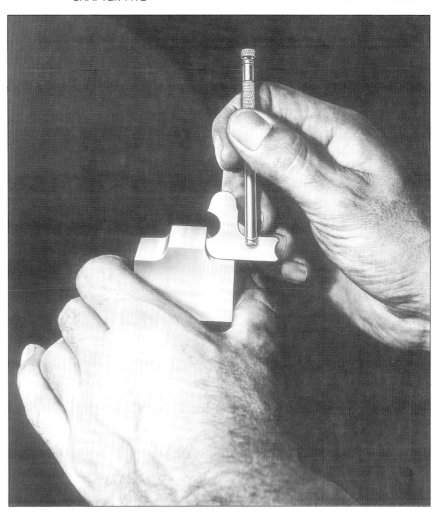

Fixed radius gauges are simply templates that are set in place and the fit with the machined curvature checked by eyeball. A clamp-on holder aids aligning the gauge correctly, helping to avoid tilting that would throw the gauging off. *L.S. Starrett Company*

pitch, and the pitch diameter. The major diameter is the dimension across the outside diameter of the threads, and can be measured with a micrometer. The minor diameter can be measured with fair but never absolute accuracy with a Vernier or dial caliper having suitably thin, knife-edged jaws that will actually reach down to the minor diameter without interfering with the flanks of the threads. The pitch can be checked using a simple thread pitch gauge, as mentioned above, or can be established by simply laying a rule beside the threads and counting.

The most critical dimension of a screw thread is the pitch diameter. Technically, this is the diameter of an imaginary cylinder whose surface intersects the threads at a point where the widths of the empty spaces are exactly equal to the widths of the threads. There are numerous procedures for measuring pitch diameter; the "three-wire" method described below is quite practical and perhaps the most appropriate for our purposes.

The principle of the three-wire method is easily understood from the adjacent illustration. At first glance, it might seem that the

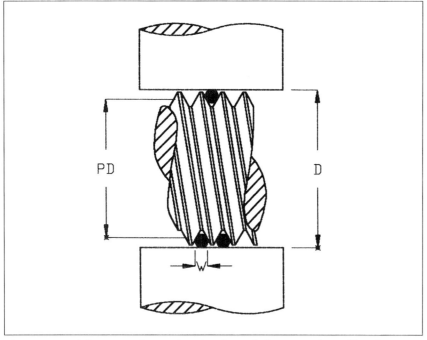

The most critical dimension of screw threads is the pitch diameter, indicated here by "PD." While there are quicker methods that may not be as accurate, and some slightly more accurate methods that are far more difficult, the "three-wire" method described in the text is commonly used for this measurement. The dimension "D," across the outside of the wires, is gauged with a micrometer, as is the diameter of the wires themselves.

A drawback to the three-wire method of gauging thread pitch diameter is the need for umpteen sets of fingers to hold everything in place during the measurement. A simple holder for the wires turns this into a easy one-man job. *Brown & Sharpe, North Kingston, RI*

diameter of the wire used here is absolutely critical. In fact, useful information can be gained using wire of any diameter that will enter between the thread flanks, yet not drop fully into the root. Nevertheless, there is only one wire diameter that will contact the thread flanks exactly at the theoretical pitch diameter. For any Unified National thread, that ideal diameter is given by the following formula:

$$W = 0.57735 \times P$$

where:

W = ideal wire diameter, inches

P = pitch, inches

For example, the ideal wire diameter for a thread with a pitch of 28 tpi is:

$$W = 0.57735 \times 1/28$$
$$= 0.0206 \text{ inch}$$

More critical than a slight variation from this ideal wire diameter is that the wire be truly round and, over 1/4 inch at least, straight, both within 0.0002 inch.

The theoretical pitch diameter for any given external thread can be looked up in any standard machinist's handbook, such as *Machinery's Handbook*, published by The Industrial Press, Inc., N.Y. The *actual* pitch diameter measured by the above method is given by the following formula:

$$PD = D + (0.86603 \times P) - (3 \times W)$$

where:

PD = pitch diameter, inches

D = micrometer measurement across wires, inches

P = pitch, inches

W = wire diameter, inches

For example, using the ideal wire diameter obtained above, the value measured by micrometer across a 1/4-28 bolt that is claimed to be a Class 3A fit (the "A" stands for external threads; internal threads are identified as "B") might be 0.2548 inch. The pitch diameter then is:

$$PD = 0.2548 + (0.86603 \times 1/28) - (3 \times .0206)$$
$$= 0.2548 + (0.03093) - (0.0618)$$
$$= 0.22393, \text{ or, rounding to four places } 0.2239$$

The book value for pitch diameter on a 1/4-28 UNF Class 3A thread is 0.2243–0.2268. Therefore, the pitch diameter is undersize; the bolt will be a loose fit . . . more like Class 2A.

As an alternative to the above, special thread gauging micrometers are available, having a conical tip on the spindle and a double-toothed profile on the anvil; the "teeth" on the anvil straddle one thread, while the pointed anvil enters the gap opposite. Clearly, any single instrument can only cover a small range of thread pitches, so several such mikes are needed.

C
O
N
T
E
N
T
S

Mechanical Weight
Scales (Balances) 78

Electronic Weigh Scales . . 81

Force Gauges 83

Torque Wrenches 86

Using a Torque Wrench . . 91

Measuring Pressures
and Vacuum 92

The "U"-Tube
Manometer 92

Other Pressure Gauges . . 94

Leak-Down Testers 97

MEASURING WEIGHTS, FORCES, AND PRESSURES

Every material thing in the universe has a certain amount of "stuff" in it—it has a certain mass. Just how much that stuff *weighs*, however, depends on where we do the measuring. For example, a certain astronaut who weighs, say, 180 pounds on earth would weigh only 30 pounds on the moon. Standing in an elevator that is accelerating upward, on the other hand, he might weigh 200 pounds. Yet that individual surely contains exactly the same amount of "stuff" no matter where he is.

Mass, then, is a fixed property of an object, and does not vary. Weight, on the other hand, is the effect certain external influences such as gravity have on that mass, and because those influences can vary, the weight of a fixed mass can vary too. Even the international reference kilogram—that chunk of platinum-iridium alloy held at the International Bureau of Weights and Measures in Paris—would weigh a little more than 1 kilogram at the North Pole, and a little less at the equator, because the force of gravity varies about 1/2 of 1 percent from point-to-point over the surface of the earth. (It is said that Formula One teams, who race all over the globe, have to take this variation into account. Also, for this reason, in most jurisdictions, a weigh-scale used for trade is only certified to be accurate for its listed location.)

Still, the variation in the pull of gravity between one location and another is very slight, so for real world purposes there is little need to draw this distinction very tightly. One reason to do so here, however, is because in common usage the same units (pounds, in most of our experience) are used not just for weight and mass but also for *force*. So, the 180-pound "weight" we ascribe to our imaginary space man is, in fact, the *force* that appears as a result of earth's gravity acting on his mass. In the same way, the force exerted on a wheel rim by a 1-ounce wheel weight could amount to umpteen pounds when the wheel is rotating at high speed.

Mechanical Weight Scales (Balances)

The most direct way to measure the weight of something, and arguably the most accurate way, is to balance it against the known weight of a reference mass, using a rocking beam, like a teeter-totter. This is ages-old technology—it dates back about 7,000 years, to the ancient Egyptians—and is also the only method of weighing whose accuracy is independent of where on earth we do the measuring. The accuracy of the result obtained by balancing depends only on the quality of the swivel joint, the accuracy of the reference weight(s), and the exact placement of the two masses relative to the hinge point.

These issues are well addressed by the traditional lab balance. A very low-friction swivel is achieved by using a hardened steel knife edge rocking on an agate (jewel) bearing. The distance from the fulcrum to the points of loading depends on the accuracy of linear measurement achieved by the manufacturer, and such measurements can be very accurate indeed. (Anyway, this last factor can be checked by swapping the weights between pans; if the scale balances both ways, it proves that both the weights and the arm lengths are equal.)

Finally, reference weight(s) can be purchased in several degrees of accuracy, up to National Bureau of Standards Class S (lab reference grade), which allows a tolerance of no more than 2.5 milligrams (mg) on a 1-kilogram weight—2.5 parts per million, about the same as a gauge block! Notably, though, while simple beam balances are quite inexpensive, a high-accuracy set of weights is not. A set of certified Class S weights from 5 milligrams to 100 grams can cost two or three times as much as even a top quality balance. Conversely, Class C or F ("student" grade) weights spanning the same range can be had for about the price of a six-pack of beer. Heavier reference weights can be purchased individually.

Quite apart from their cost, the need to select a combination of reference weights exactly matching the unknown weight can be tedious. Accordingly, even the cheapest laboratory balance sold these days has a sliding weight that can be moved along the beam to various positions; this modification produces what is known as a *beam balance*. Ordinary laboratory beam balances typically

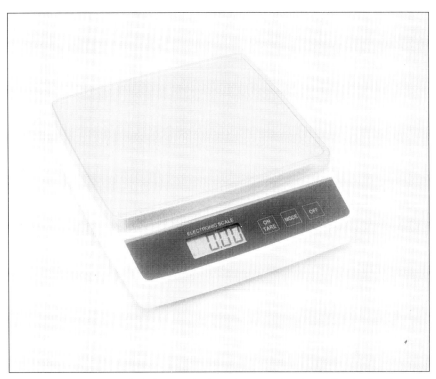

Mechanical balances and platform scales have been rendered virtually obsolete by electronic weigh scales. The applications of this technology range from sensitive laboratory "balances" (they don't actually balance anymore), to systems designed to weigh several tons. In between are parts-weighing units with a capacity of a few pounds, like this one. *Intercomp Co.*

have a beam with 0.1-gram divisions and a total range of 10 grams. To extend the range of the tool, fixed weights can be added to one pan, up to the maximum capacity of the balance, usually 2 kilograms (about 4 1/2 pounds).

Just as there is a practical limit to the "fineness" of the divisions on a steel rule, there is some irreducible minimum distance between the markings for the sliding weight on a beam balance. Thus, the size of the step between one division and the next depends on the size of the sliding weight. For any given length of beam, a heavier sliding weight will increase the total range of the instrument, but will reduce its precision. To deal with this, more than one beam can be provided, each with its own sliding weight, ranging from "light" to "heavy." Using this prin-

ciple, which gives us "double beam" and "triple beam" balances, the range of weights that can be measured can be greatly expanded, without the need for loose weights.

The beam balance principle can be extended to just about any total weight capacity, but large-capacity, high-accuracy units become impractically large. To circumvent this, large-capacity mechanical platform scales use arrangements of compound levers, to give the sliding reference weight(s) more mechanical advantage. Inevitably, the added number of bearing points, plus potential slight errors in the lengths of the levers, threatens accuracy.

Other drawbacks to using the balance principle to weigh things are the susceptibility of the jeweled swivel(s) to damage and sensitivity to sideways-acting loads. (Scales of all sorts are somewhat affected by

This roughly 2x3x8-inch block of aluminum is the "spring" in the load cell of an electronic wheel scale. The cell is fastened to the base only at the rear, while the pad is bolted only to the front, which sits slightly above the base (note the postcard in between). A force applied to the pad thus tends to bend the cell in the middle, where some of it is machined away. The pencil points at the location of the strain gauge, protected here by a rubber cover, that measures the deflection of the block. *Robin Harford photo, courtesy* Stock Car Racing *magazine*

This electronic hanging scale weighs up to 750 pounds, in 0.1-pound increments, with 0.1 percent accuracy; similar units are available to 1,000 pounds. The display can also be configured to read in kilograms. *Intercomp Co.*

percent of the indicated value—1 part in 1,000.

(Note here that accuracy can be expressed relative to the indicated value or to the full scale reading, sometimes abbreviated to "percentage FS." The potential inaccuracy of any measuring tool that has its accuracy expressed as a "percentage FS" gets larger as the measured value gets smaller. A spring scale with a maximum rating of 500 pounds and a claimed accuracy of plus-or-minus 2 percent FS may be in error by 2 percent of 500—i.e., 10 pounds—at *any* weight. Thus, an indicated weight of 100 pounds could, in fact, be anywhere between 90 pounds and 110 pounds!)

Electronic Weigh Scales

Weighing by measuring the extension of a spring is also the operating principle of most electronic weigh scales which, paradoxically, can be at least as accurate as a sensitive mechanical balance. Electronic digital scales come in all sizes from electronic lab "balances" that measure in units of milligrams—one-millionth of a kilogram—to railroad weigh scales that can cope with several hundred tons.

In these applications, the spring is not obvious, but it is there nonetheless, in the form of a *load cell*. This comprises a specially shaped metal part—the "spring"—that actually bears the load, plus an electronic strain gauge that measures the deflection of the "spring." Load cells, too, face the same problems of nonuniform spring rate and

side forces.) As well, even if the movement of the balancing beam is damped, a considerable amount of time can be occupied in waiting for things to "settle down," as the beam gently tilts back and forth.

As a result of all these considerations, alternative methods of weighing have been developed. It turns out that most of these alternatives boil down, ultimately, to measuring the extension of a spring. In postal, bathroom, and fisherman's scales, the spring is obvious. Ordinary spring scales of this class are notoriously inaccurate, however, partly because these

mass-market products are cheaply made, but also because of the extreme difficulty of producing a spring that extends exactly equal amounts for every equal increase in load. Simple springs are also sensitive to temperature changes.

According to one manufacturer of certified weigh scales, a total error of up to 5 percent of the full scale reading is not uncommon for the grade of spring-type scale you might buy in the local hardware store. This is why they are marked "Not Legal for Trade." In most jurisdictions, the standard of accuracy required for trade is ± 0.1

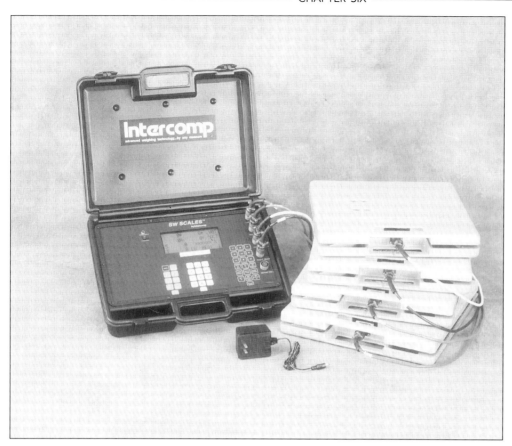

Adjusting individual wheel weights is an important step in race car chassis setup, and for that wheel scales are needed. Mechanical scales with the required capacity would be huge and heavy; electronic wheel scales are portable, and accurate to 0.1 percent of the indicated value. Their electronic output is fed to a single-purpose electronic calculator that can report not just individual weights and a total but also front-to-rear and side-to-side distribution, expressed as percentages. *Intercomp Co.*

temperature sensitivity as any other scale based on spring deflection. Still, the first source of error is reduced, because the spring is very stiff and never moves very far, and both this factor and the temperature problem can be largely corrected by the internal electronics that convert the output of the strain gauge into a numerical display. Commercial electronic scales in the range of, say, 10 pounds to 100,000 pounds, typically have an accuracy of 0.1 percent of the applied load. Other sources of error that *cannot* easily be electronically compensated are "creep" (a tendency for the reading to change over time) and "zero drift"—the amount that the zero point changes over time.

Although it is fewer than 30 years since they first became widely available, electronic weigh scales have almost completely replaced the earlier mechanical methods in industry, and especially in retail marketing, because the electronic output from any number of scales can be fed into a computer system. This has slashed the price of these once-expensive instruments; now, most of the weight and force measuring tools offered to the automotive market are of this type. In addition to parts scales with a capacity of about 3 kilograms (say 7 pounds) and hanging scales up to about 1,000-pound capacity, many race teams use electronic platform-type scales to determine the weights supported by individual wheels, to aid in chassis setup.

Here, advantage is taken of the electrical nature of the load cell's output to allow various related calculations to be performed by a computer, generally supplied with the scales. By use of four scales connected to one "black box," front-to-rear and side-to-side weight distribution can be displayed, both expressed as percentages, as well as all four individual weights, plus the total. Some systems offer even more advanced calculating features.

Individual "pads" generally have a capacity of 1,500 pounds, for a total system capacity of 6,000 pounds; most claim an accuracy of 0.1 percent. In an independent test conducted by *Open Wheel* magazine, technical editor Doug Gore found three of four makes of electronic wheel scales to be well within these accuracy limits when tested with a known 610-pound weight. Static error and repeatability was within 2 pounds or less, as was the variation between tests at

40 degrees and at 85 degrees Fahrenheit. A rather larger error, about 0.75 percent, arose from applying a side load (size unknown).

Remember that any sort of weigh scale is actually measuring the force of gravity acting on whatever is being weighed, and gravity acts straight downward. For accuracy, then, the scale must be perfectly level.

Force Gauges

Weighing is nothing more than a special case of measuring a force, so it should come as no surprise that tools for measuring force use exactly the same principles as those for measuring weight.

As it turns out, about the only forces of interest to us are those developed by springs, particularly road (wheel) springs and valve and clutch springs. A handful of devices on the market measure the force exerted by a spring at any given amount of deflection. Comparing that force at several different deflections allows us to determine a spring's rate. Capacities for road spring rate checkers vary from 2,000 pounds to 5,000 pounds, with electronic models usually having 1-pound increments; smaller tools such as for valve springs have capacities of 500 to 1,000 pounds, usually in 0.1-pound increments.

Commercially available road spring rate checkers comprise a sturdy steel frame with a fixed but adjustable abutment for the spring under test at the top, and a platform at the bottom that can be raised with a hydraulic bottle jack, so compressing the spring by a controllable amount.

According to brand and model, the travel of the lower platform may be registered by a simple rule-type scale, by a dial indicator, or by a digital electronic travel indicator.

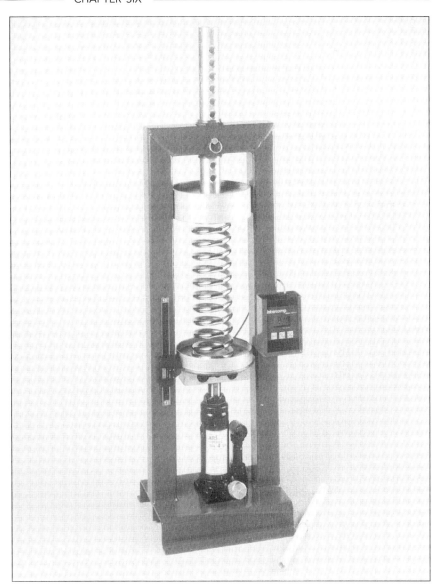

Road spring checkers resemble an arbor press. As the spring is compressed by the bottle jack, its travel is indicated by the scale on the left, while the force can be read from the display on the right. In this case, both travel and force are gauged electronically. *Intercomp Co.*

The method of measuring the force applied to the spring also varies. The simplest scheme is to connect a pressure gauge to the hydraulic jack; the alternative, at nearly twice the price, is a load cell sandwiched between the spring and the lower platform.

The "hydraulic" arrangement entails a couple of possible problem areas. First, conventional English system pressure gauges are calibrated in pounds per square inch (psi). Now, ideally, the numbers on the gauge should directly report the force on the spring in pounds, but for this to work out, the hydraulic cylinder has to have an area of exactly 1 square inches, which in turn requires a bore of 1.1284 inch. Ordinary hydraulic jacks, though, usually have cylinders that are some common inch-fractional size, such as 1 inch or 1 1/4 inches.

There are three ways around this problem: You can calculate the

While their measurement by electronic means has strong advantages, spring forces and travel can be gauged without the use of electronics. This unit (not a current production item) uses a hydraulic pressure gauge to read the pressure within the jack, which is proportional to the force applied. The travel is shown by a long-range dial indicator. *Longacre Automotive Racing Products*

With smaller spring forces (to, say, 1,000 pounds), it is practical to apply the load mechanically, through a screw jack. This unit is intended for checking valve, clutch, or other similar springs with ± 0.25 percent accuracy. Both force and travel are detected and displayed digitally. *Intercomp Co.*

force based on the indicated pressure and the measured diameter of the piston in the jack; you can interpose a second hydraulic piston-and-cylinder with a 1.1284 inch bore between the bottom platform and the jack, and feed the pressure gauge from there; or you can produce a new face for the pressure gauge.

Whichever of these methods is used, there is a second problem: To contain umpteen hundred psi requires a mighty snug-fitting seal in the jack (or in the hydraulic "sensing" cell), and that seal is certain to have a considerable amount of friction. Unless the dial face has been directly calibrated using known weights, the pressure gauge will invariably read high by an unknown amount.

Because the cost of the load cell drops significantly as the maximum load decreases, many of the similar but smaller tools used for valve, clutch, pressure relief springs, etc., do use a load cell. One such unit with a capacity of 1,000 pounds, displayed in 0.1-pound increments, claims a commendable plus-or-minus 0.25 percent accuracy.

A handful of spring force measuring tools, generally intended for checking valve springs, operate purely mechanically. Some are designed for use on an assembled engine, to determine the "on-the-seat" force of valve springs; others are for bench use. All of these work by pitting the test spring against another, calibrated, one. Usually the calibrated spring is a flat beam that bends when the operator uses the tool to apply a force to the spring. A pointer attached to the working end indicates the applied force on some sort of scale. The accuracy of these tools is not high—one popular brand of

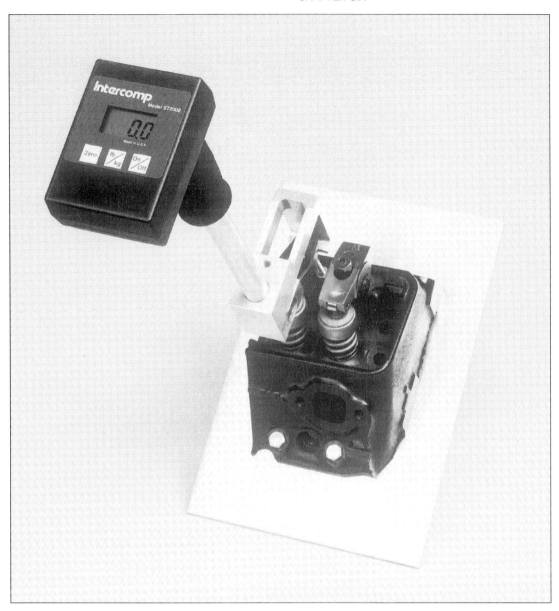

When the added accuracy justifies the expense, an alternative to the tool in the previous picture is an electronic digital version. This one reads in 0.1-pound increments. *Intercomp Co.*

This is a purely mechanical tool for gauging on-the-seat valve spring force. When the user applies force to the handle, a flat blade spring bends; as it does so, the force applied is read off the curved scale. *Moroso Performance Products, Inc.*

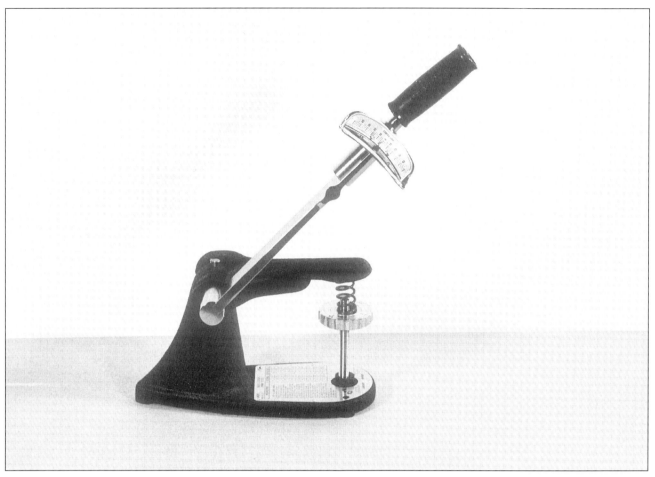

The original device, and perhaps the simplest, for measuring the forces exerted by small springs, particularly valve springs, is this tool that uses a torque wrench as the calibrated spring and scale. *Sturtevant-Richmond Division, Ryeson Corp.*

on-the-engine valve spring seat force checker, for instance, has a claimed accuracy of plus-or-minus 3 percent. The original form of mechanical small spring tester amounts to a test fixture intended for use with a torque wrench. The wrench supplies the calibrated spring and scale.

Torque Wrenches

To do their job properly, bolts and screws have to be tightened to some extent. This is often understood to be to prevent their loosening through vibration, but there is another, more important, reason, especially in the case of critical, highly loaded engine bolts.

The loads on many of these

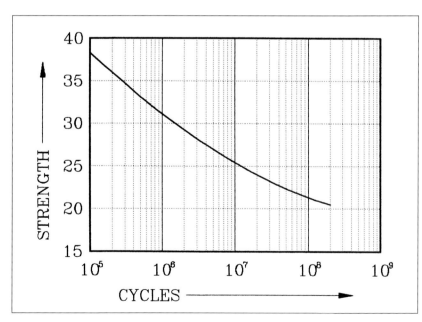

Metals that experience fluctuating loads grow weaker over time—they *fatigue*. Their strength after a few million cycles of on-again-off-again loading is only a fraction of the size of constantly applied load they could have withstood when new. The effect grows worse as the size of the variation increases.

fasteners fluctuate. Connecting rod bolts, for example, get tugged violently every time the piston reaches the top of the cylinder, then they get to rest, then get jerked again. Now, a varying load like this causes metals to fatigue—they gradually grow weaker over time—and the severity of that effect depends on how wide the variation is. Oddly, it turns out that one way to reduce this tendency to fatigue is to prevent the bolt from ever completely relaxing, so the fatigue life of a bolt—how many stress-relax cycles it will tolerate—depends greatly on how tightly it is fastened in the first place. The usual aim of engineers is to preload a tension bolt to 80 percent of its yield strength, and all the various tables of torque values for tightening critical fasteners are based on that assumption.

Federal standards allow torque wrenches a reading error of 4 percent between 20 percent and 100 percent of wrench capacity. Below 20 percent, they allow an error of 0.8 percent of *full scale*. At the same time, repeatedly using the wrench above 80 percent of its nominal capacity may cause it to gradually creep out of calibration, as whatever serves as the spring element takes on a permanent "set." It is important, then, to choose a wrench so it will operate somewhere near the middle of its range. Both inch and metric tools are available in a very wide range of capacities, so there should be no problem in "sizing" the wrench.

The simplest, least expensive, and most rugged and reliable torque wrenches involve a straight beam that connects the handle to the square drive. As the beam bends under load, a pointer attached to the head of the square drive indicates the equivalent applied torque on a scale attached

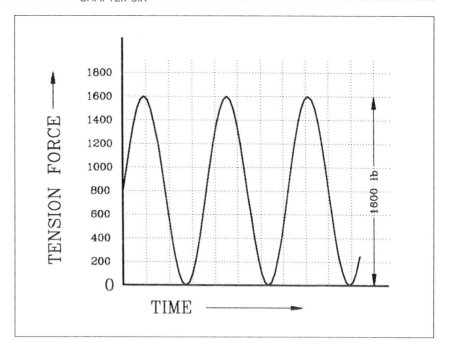

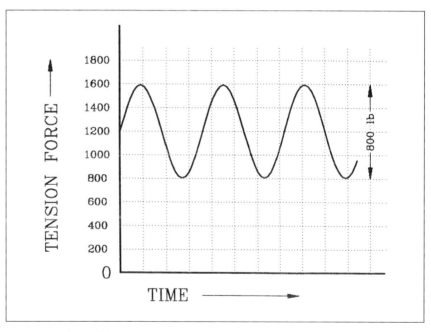

One way to forestall fatigue is to prevent a part from ever really relaxing. By preloading a bolt, for example, to half the peak load it will see, the variation in load between "on" and "off" is cut in half.

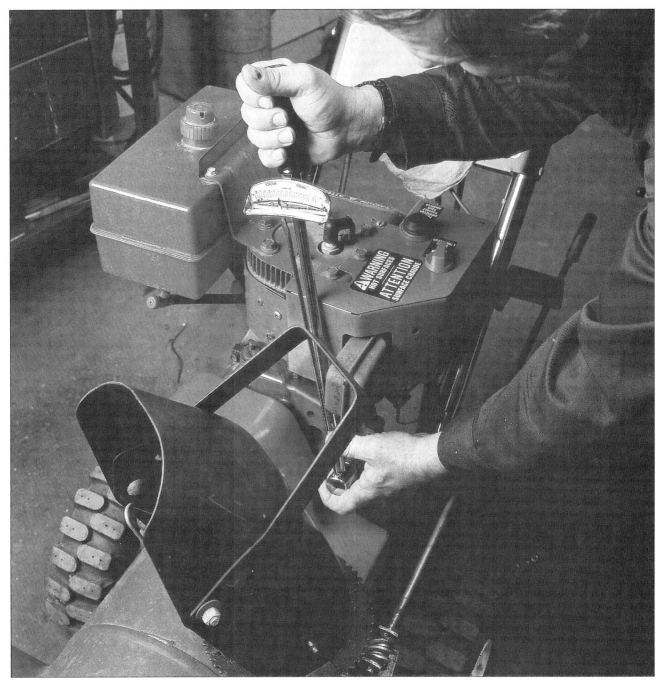

Tightening during installation produces a preload in a bolt, so its tendency to fatigue is reduced. Too much initial preload, however, will break it. One way to control preload is by carefully regulating the initial torquing. The most common way to gauge that torquing is with a torque wrench. The earliest, simplest, and cheapest kind of torque wrench is the familiar bending beam type. *Sturtevant-Richmond Division, Ryeson Corp.*

to the handle end. These tools are fairly accurate, typically plus-or-minus 2 percent; higher accuracy units can cut that in half. What is more, they are likely to remain accurate even if somewhat abused. (It is quite permissible to rebend a

pointer that gets knocked askew; just gently bend it back so it points at the zero mark on the scale.)

A drawback to this class of tool is the need for the user to ensure that his force is applied to the swivel where the handle attaches to

the beam—an incorrect "grip" can lead to errors. Also, while some models have a "tell-tale" that indicates the highest reading, with others it is necessary to both tighten and watch the scale at the same time.

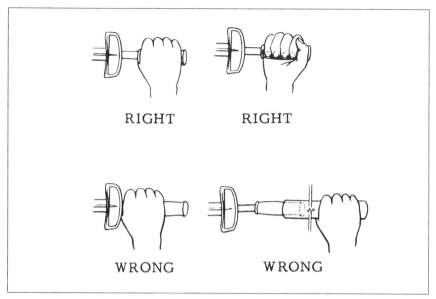

RIGHT   RIGHT

WRONG   WRONG

A drawback to the simple bending beam torque wrench is the need to ensure the force is applied at a specific distance from the drive end. A precisely located swivel at the handle fixes that point, but the user needs to ensure that the handle is free to "float" around that swivel. Not always easy. *Sturtevant-Richmond Division, Ryeson Corp.*

Dial-type torque wrenches are usually based on a torsion spring arrangement at the drive end, so directly read the torque applied, no matter where the wrench is gripped. This advantage over the bending beam type may be to some extent offset by the smaller (and thus less easily read) scale on the dial face, and by the higher cost. *Sturtevant-Richmond Division, Ryeson Corp.*

Other common types avoid these operational drawbacks. Dial-type wrenches are not particularly fussy where the wrench is held and have a "tell-tale" that remains at the highest reading achieved. Accuracy is comparable to a beam-type tool (plus-or-minus 2 percent for common models, 1 percent for precision units), but may prove harder to *read* accurately because the scale is smaller than on a beam-type tool.

"Click"-type wrenches have a twist grip on the end of the handle with markings around its circumference that indicate the preset level of torque. Turning this adjuster compresses a strong coil spring that opposes the endwise movement of a shoe resting on a shaped cam connected to the square drive (all of this hidden inside the tool). When the preset value is reached, the shoe slips over the cam with a "click" that can be both heard and felt. There are also other working principles. As a rule, this class of wrench is less accurate than either the beam or dial types, one brand-name unit being within plus-or-minus 4 percent when used clockwise, plus-or-minus 6 percent counter-clockwise.

There is a problem here, however. The relationship between the torque applied to the head of a bolt and the tension produced in the bolt as a result of that torquing can vary widely, depending on surface smoothness of the threads, type of plating, lubrication, and other factors. So, no matter how accurately it might measure *torque*, a torque wrench cannot control the tension in a bolt with an accuracy of better than about ± 25 percent. To avoid overloading the bolt during installation, torque table figures have to assume the high end of that ± 25 percent.

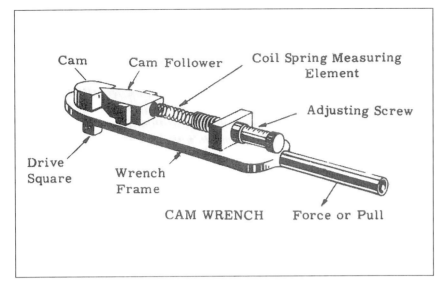

Cam   Cam Follower   Coil Spring Measuring Element

Adjusting Screw

Drive Square   Wrench Frame

CAM WRENCH   Force or Pull

Another sort of torque wrench is the "click" type. One mechanism used is shown here. The torque at the head that it takes to force the cam follower to slip over the cam depends on the preload in the coil spring. That, in turn, is set by the user by turning the adjusting screw, usually a knurled grip at the handle. These tend to be less accurate than other types. *Sturtevant-Richmond Division, Ryeson Corp.*

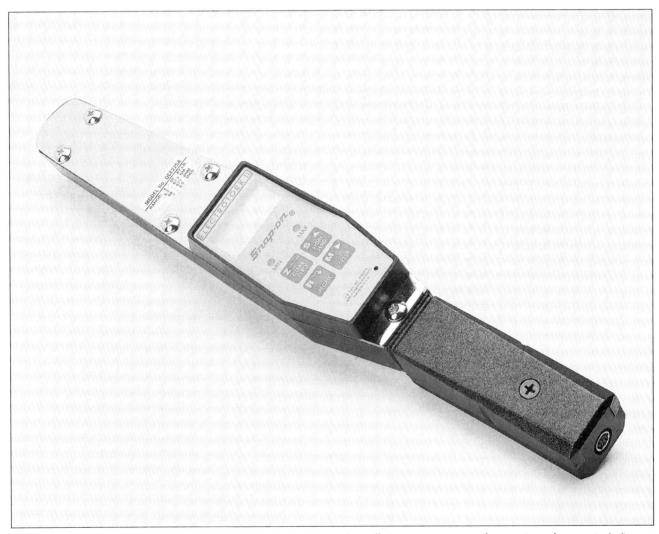

Electronics has infiltrated the torque wrench business, too. Electronics allow offering an assortment of convenience features, including an internal memory that can store numerous torque values, but they are no more accurate than other types. *Snap-on Tools Co.*

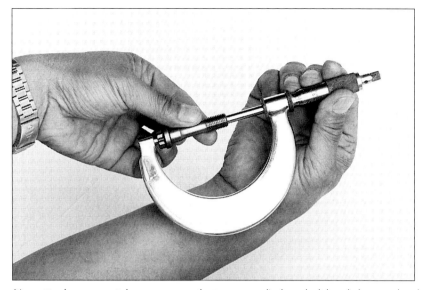

No matter how accurately you measure the torque applied to a bolt head, the actual preload in the bolt can vary widely, depending on materials, lubrication, etc. The only way to directly gauge the preload is to measure the stretch in the fastener. First, carefully measure the free length of the bolt (left), and record the figure. During installation (right), torque the bolt until it has stretched the amount specified in the bolt maker's instructions. The stretch can be measured by micrometer or, as here, with a dial gauge. *Automotive Racing Products*

While there are some sophisticated techniques for measuring the tensile stress in a bolt more directly, for our purposes, the only direct way to determine the tension preload in a bolt is to calculate the exact amount of stretch that the required preload will cause, then to measure the free length of the bolt using a Vernier micrometer, and to tighten it during installation until it has grown longer by exactly the appropriate amount. This is by far the most accurate and reliable method of controlling preload, and is the only method that should be used for the most critical fasteners, especially connecting rod bolts. Unfortunately, this technique only works when we have access to both ends of the bolt. In other cases, there is no practical alternative to a torque wrench, so it is worth saying a few words about its use.

Using a Torque Wrench

The enormous local forces in the threads when a bolt is tightened into a tapped hole or nut actually smooth the worst of the surface irregularities—the high spots literally get squashed flatter. That is why a bolt that is torqued hard once and then rechecked later will be found to have "relaxed." Similarly, the act of running a bolt into and out of the mating female threads tends to burnish the surface, so the torque-to-tension relationship changes. Again, the act of tightening one bolt in a pattern changes the load on the other bolts in the pattern, as the part being bolted warps around.

For all these reasons, and others, bolts should be torqued in steps. One accepted practice is to first install every bolt in a pattern just snug, then torque them all, using a criss-cross pattern to, say, 50 percent of the final figure. Then work up to 75 percent or 80 percent. At this point it is wise to let the joint "settle," to give time for the high local stresses on the thread surfaces to relax. Finally, bring all the fasteners up to the final figure. Some painstaking mechanics go further, especially when working with brand-new fasteners. They will loosen the fasteners after the 50 percent tightening, run them all the way out, then start over again. This, it is hoped, will burnish the new surfaces, improving the uniformity of the torque-tension relationship.

Because of the wide variations in this relationship, be sure that whatever torque figure you may be working to is appropriate to the particular combination of factors that apply in your case. Use a manufacturer's or supplier's figures in preference to a "universal" torque table whenever possible.

The working end of torque wrenches customarily terminates in a square drive—usually 3/8 inch or 1/2 inch, although some small-capacity wrenches use a 1/4-inch drive—for attachment of sockets, screwdriver tips, etc. When some other sort of device is needed to

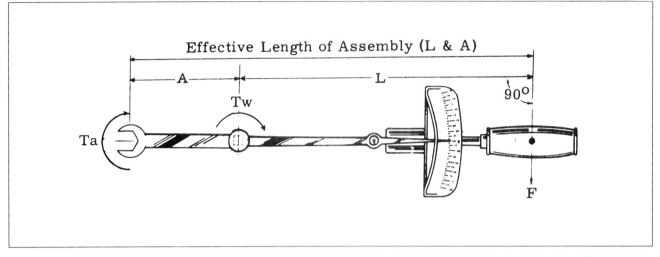

Any adapter that adds distance between the square drive and the fastener will make any type of torque wrench read "low." Multiply the reading (or setting) on the wrench by the proportional increase in overall length. *Sturtevant-Richmond Division, Ryeson Corp.*

engage with the work, such as an open-end wrench attachment to reach into awkward spaces, the effective length of the wrench is increased. This has to be taken into account when relating the torque actually applied to the fastener to the number on the wrench scale. In practice, the torque at the fastener is equal to the indicated torque on the wrench scale, multiplied by the proportional increase in length. For example, an adapter that measures one-quarter of the length of the wrench (as measured from the center of the square drive to the handle swivel, in the case of beam-type wrenches) increases the torque at the fastener head by 25 percent over the reading on the wrench scale.

If you simply cannot develop enough grunt to achieve a desired torque reading, get a bigger wrench . . . *do not* attempt to increase the leverage with a length of pipe. While this may not, in the case of dial- or "click"-type wrenches, result in an erroneous reading, it will surely mean work-

ing the wrench right at the top of its range, which is not a good idea. In the case of beam-type wrenches, it will result in a large but incalculable error.

Measuring Pressures and Vacuum

Pressure is simply an expression of force per unit of area. Thus, a pressure of 20 psi within a closed container (a tire, a fuel line, a cooling system) means that a force of 20 pounds acts on each square inch of the interior surface of the container.

The measurement of vacuum is very much the same thing. Note that a "pure" vacuum, such as exists in space, is essentially impossible to achieve on earth. The vacuum in the intake manifold of a running engine, for example, is actually some small positive pressure, relative to a perfect vacuum. We will take a "vacuum" to be any pressure below local atmospheric pressure. (See also the sidebar "Sucking and Blowing.")

Because a pressure is simply a force applied over some reference

area, a pressure gauge is actually measuring force, so its internal workings again often employ one of the same principles used to measure weight or force.

The "U"-Tube Manometer

A very simple tool for measuring the pressure of a gas or liquid is the *manometer*. A manometer is just a transparent glass or plastic tube bent into a U-shape, with a quantity of fluid trapped in the "U." At rest, atmospheric pressure bears down equally on the top of the column of fluid on each side of the "U." When an external pressure is applied to one side of the "U," some of the fluid is pushed upward into the other side, until the weight of the extra fluid just balances the "push" exerted by the external pressure. The difference in height between the fluid in the two sides of the "U" thus indicates the applied pressure.

While commercially made manometers are available, complete with finely etched graduations on the tubes, many folks who use these things in their shop work find it

The ability to accurately measure pressure and differences between one zone and another is fundamental to flow bench work. The tall, vertically oriented mercury manometers at the left will span one atmosphere or so. The smaller inclined manometer (probably water-filled) allows very precise reading of small pressure differences. *Doug Gore photo, courtesy* Open Wheel *magazine*

easy (and much cheaper!) to make their own, using a simple rule for the measurement of the difference in the fluid column heights.

A manometer can also be used to measure a pressure *below* atmospheric, in which case it becomes a vacuum gauge. Here, it is the atmospheric side of the "U" tube that does the pushing; the fluid will rise in the other, "vacuum" side of the "U," indicating the pressure difference between the two sides.

Of course, if there is sufficient pressure difference between the two sides of the "U" tube, the fluid will get blown completely out. The total range of the instrument thus depends on its overall height; it also depends on the density of the fluid in the "U." If we use ordinary water, for example, a mere 1-psi difference between the two sides will result in the water column in one side being roughly 28 inches higher than the other; just one standard atmosphere of pressure will support a column of water nearly 34 feet tall. So, the height of instrument required for measuring anything above some fraction of an atmosphere becomes completely impractical.

By the same token, a water-filled manometer can offer very fine measurement of low pressures, and this capability can be further expanded by inclining the tubes at an angle, so that a small change in vertical height involves a substantial distance along the manometer tube. This technique is sometimes used when measuring the small pressure drops through an engine's intake system; people who rework ports or carburetor venturis often work with inclined water manometers.

When using water (and many other fluids) in this way, a complication that enters is the surface tension of the fluid. The same physical property that makes water dripping from a tap gather up into droplets also causes its surface, when confined in a surrounding tube, to

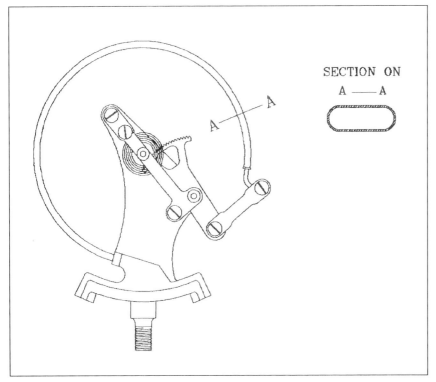

SECTION ON
A —— A

The basic "works" of most mechanical pressure gauges is a Bourdon tube. The curved, closed-end tube is oval in cross section, so internal pressure tends to make the oval bulge into a circle. That, in turn, makes the overall curvature straighten out. Movement of the free end of the tube is amplified by a gear train, to drive the pointer.

The highest pressures encountered in automotive work are those in the brake system. Pressure of 1,500 psi or more can arise under "panic" braking. A gauge spanning from zero to 1,500 will have its markings crammed very close together, reducing precision. Whatever the *accuracy* of a gauge, its precision always diminishes as its maximum reading is increased. *Moroso Performance Products, Inc.*

become bent, creating what is called a *meniscus curve*—the surface bulges up at the edges. This makes it difficult to determine just how high in the tube the surface actually is. With water, the fix for this is to add just a drop or two of liquid dishwashing detergent, greatly reducing the surface tension and so almost eliminating the meniscus. A dash of food coloring greatly aids reading the top of the fluid column.

For measuring somewhat higher pressures with a U-tube manometer, we need a fluid that is denser than water. The densest fluid available to us is mercury, and this makes for a manometer of practical length when measuring pressures around one atmosphere. Nevertheless, one atmosphere pressure difference across a mercury-filled U-tube manometer still entails a column nearly 30 inches tall. When much larger pressures need to be measured, the overall height of manometer needed becomes impractically large, so other means are used.

Other Pressure Gauges

By far the most common type of purely mechanical pressure gauge is the *Bourdon tube* type. In this, the fluid under pressure fills a curved, closed-ended tube. Increases in pressure tend to straighten out the tube, causing its free end to move. This movement is then amplified by a series of gears, with the output being connected to the pointer. Clearly, this is force measuring based on the spring-extension principle, the spring being the tube itself. Virtually all mechanical pressure gauges use the Bourdon tube principle, but their accuracies vary widely, mostly according to the amount of care that goes into producing the curved tube. Inexpensive

Bourdon tube mechanical gauges have an accuracy of about 2.5 percent FS; high-precision ones may be 1 percent FS or better; lab quality reference gauges are available with a certified accuracy of 0.1 percent FS.

The range of pressures we might encounter is surprisingly wide. The pressure in the "slicks" on a drag car, for instance, might be as little as 4-5 psig (psi, gauge), while the hydraulic pressure in that same car's brake lines can exceed 1,500 psig. Such a span obviously cannot be coped with by any single gauge, and careful thought needs to go into considering the maximum pressure a gauge will be used to measure; choosing one with a higher capacity will inevitably reduce both precision and accuracy. A larger diameter face eases readability, and thus the accuracy of the reading, though it says nothing directly about the accuracy of the gauge itself.

The tool suppliers who advertise in automotive magazines offer mechanical (Bourdon tube) tire pressure gauges typically in three ranges: 0–15 psig, 0–50 psig (or 0–60 psig), and 0–100 psig. When accuracy is not specified, you can assume it is 2 percent FS or worse; some precision units are available

Sucking and Blowing: Units of Pressure

In the whole world of metrology—the science and technology of measurement—the measurement of pressure is surely more capable of causing bewilderment than any other physical quantity. Where the confusion arises is in the mind-boggling number of different ways that the same pressure can be expressed.

First is the issue of whether we are talking about an absolute pressure or a gauge pressure. To explain, in a perfect vacuum, as in outer space, there is no pressure at all . . . zero. Here on earth, on the other hand, the weight of all the air molecules in our atmosphere presses down on the surface of the world with a pressure of about 14.7 psi. So, a gauge that measures absolute pressure would read 14.7 psi when it is not hooked up to anything. However, most pressure gauges (but not all) actually report the pressure above atmospheric, so they would read zero under the same conditions. The terms "psig" (psi, gauge) and "psia" (psi, absolute) are used to distinguish between these two.

Another way to express absolute pressure is in terms of "atmospheres"; one atmosphere is roughly 14.7 psia. Thus two atmospheres would be 29.4 psia, or 14.7 psig; 10 atmospheres would be 147 psia, or 132.3 psig. This is a common method of expressing pressures that are rather high, if only because the units—atmospheres—are suitably large.

The traditional way that atmospheric pressure is measured (and still about the best) is with a mercury barometer. The height of the column of mercury in the tube is a measure of the local atmospheric pressure. By international agreement, a "standard atmosphere" corresponds to 29.92 inches of mercury (usually written as 29.92 in Hg . . . Hg is the chemical symbol for mercury), or 14.694 psi.

In the United States, the height of that column of mercury is described in inches; most everywhere else in the world it is expressed in millimeters. Inches (or millimeters) of mercury is also used to express pressures other than simply that of the surrounding atmosphere. Some folks describe the "boost" of a supercharger or turbocharger that way; manifold "vacuum" is almost always expressed that way.

When dealing with very low pressures, units of inches or millimeters of mercury become awkwardly large. Here, the same barometer principle can be applied using a column of water, rather than mercury, because water is so much less dense. One standard atmosphere corresponds to 406.78 inches of water, or 10,332.27 millimeters of water.

Reasonably enough, there are measures of pressure in the metric system that employ metric units for force and area. Instead of pounds-per-square-inch we might speak of kilograms-per-square-centimeter (kg/cm^2). If the numbers become clumsily large because the pressure is high, we could use kilograms-per-square-millimeter (kg/mm^2).

As if this wasn't bad enough, note that a "kilogram" is a mass, not a force. The official metric unit of force is the Newton (don't ask), and pressure, officially, is expressed as Newtons per square meter (N/m^2, or sometimes nt/m^2). Quite recently, one Newton per square meter has been named one "Pascal" (again, don't ask), abbreviated to "Pa." Because one Pascal is such a small unit, the multiples of thousands (giving kilo Pascals, or kPa) and sometimes millions (yielding mega Pascals, or mPa) are used. A standard atmosphere is 101.325 kPa.

So, add 'em up: psi, kg/cm^2, kg/mm^2, N/m^2 (or Pa), all of which might be "gauge" or "absolute," plus in Hg, mm Hg, in water, mm water . . . that makes no fewer than 12 different ways to express pressure, without counting the multiples like kPa and mPa . . . and there are a couple of others I haven't mentioned!

Tire gauges usually "hold" the highest reading until a release valve is operated, yet a sudden application of pressure can make the instrument "overshoot." Filling the gauge with a viscous fluid—a feature of many quality instruments—helps damp this overshoot. Quality mechanical pressure gauges can have an accuracy of ±0.5 percent. *Moroso Performance Products, Inc.*

from these sources with a claimed accuracy of 1 percent FS or even 0.5 percent FS.

Apart from convenience features such as internal illumination, one feature touted for some higher priced units is that they are "fluid-filled," usually with a silicon-based oil. While fluid filling is common for industrial gauges that are subject to pulsating pressures (the fluid helps damp wild swings of the needle and may help protect the mechanism), tire pressure does not pulsate in this way. Still, this feature is valuable in a tire gauge because unless the pressure is applied to the gauge very slowly, there is a tendency for the needle to overshoot, so the indicated value will be higher than that actually in the tire. To obtain a true reading, a little air has to be bled out, allowing the gauge to "catch" the true pressure on the way down. Damping suppresses this overshoot, and so prevents needless loss of air.

Other situations where pressure might need to be gauged include fuel, brake, cooling, and engine oiling systems, plus shop air pressure. Notably, the fluid under pressure is

different in each of these cases but, with the possible exception of fuel systems that involve methanol, none of these should present a problem to any Bourdon tube instrument. Some Bourdon tubes are made of brass, which is subject to corrosion by methanol. Other tube materials, such as stainless steel, are immune to all the fluids found in or around automobiles.

Fuel and oiling systems usually operate somewhere in the range of a few tens of psi . . . perhaps up to 100 psig. Gauges intended for trouble-shooting fuel pumps and fuel injection systems are sold by many familiar suppliers of mechanics' tools. One premium brand, for example, offers a 0–100-psi gauge calibrated in 1-psi increments and having a claimed accuracy of 1.5 percent, for about $100. Most interestingly, a gauge of similar specification but with certified 0.5 percent accuracy is available from an industrial supplier of test and measurement equipment . . . for about $85! This unit also features a mirror band aligned with the pointer tip that helps eliminate parallax. Similar units are available

to 1,000 psi; larger, even more accurate, and very much more expensive models come in ranges to an eye-watering 20,000 psig.

Digital electronic gauges covering comparable pressure ranges are also available, but those for pressures above, say, 2,000 psi or so are specialized industrial instruments with a very hefty price tag. For gauging more moderate pressures, electronic and mechanical instruments are remarkably competitive with each other.

Digital tire pressure gauges are especially popular with racers. In these, the "spring" is a thin diaphragm that bulges under the applied pressure; a strain gauge measures the amount of bulge. As suggested, the price spread between digital and mechanical tire pressure gauges of comparable accuracy is small to zero. For both types of instrument, though, the price rises sharply with increasing accuracy. In general, figure $50 for a 1 percent or 2 percent instrument of either type; 0.5 percent accuracy will cost three times that; 0.2 percent accuracy or better is only available from electronic units costing around $300. Apart from the minor issue of occasionally having a battery poop out (they last for months), the only real drawback to digital pressure gauges is the slight time—a second or two—needed for the instrument to "integrate" the reading.

If the pressure is expected to vary during the measurement, the gauge should, of course, "follow" the varying pressure. In other situations, it is a convenience if the gauge "holds" its reading after the source of pressure has been removed, until a release valve is operated. Tire pressure gauges are one example of this; compression gauges are another.

There is little useful to say

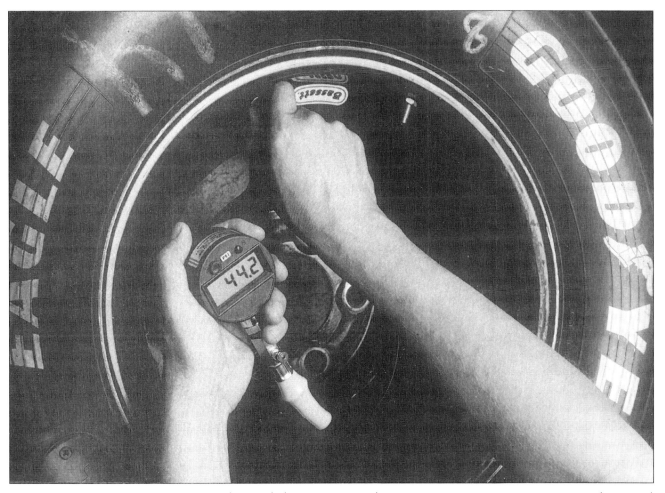

Digital tire pressure gauges are gaining in popularity. Only the most expensive, however, are any more accurate or more precise than a good mechanical gauge. As with other digital instruments, though, an advantage is the near impossibility of mis-reading. *Argo Manufacturing Co.*

about compression gauges. Accuracy is almost irrelevant, because they are mostly used to give a comparative reading between one cylinder and another, to give a rough picture of the ability of the valves and piston rings to hold pressure. The absolute accuracy hardly matters. Besides, whatever the inherent accuracy of the gauge, the actual pressure developed during cranking depends, among many other things, on the cranking speed, and that varies with battery condition. If you do a compression check on an eight-cylinder engine with a partly whacked-out battery, then recheck the first cylinder you tested, odds are good you will get a lower

reading the second time. Besides, there is a better way to perform this check—with a leak-down tester.

Leak-Down Testers

While a compression gauge can provide useful information about the internal condition of an engine, the actual numerical values it might show can be widely different from one engine to another, even though both engines are in ideal shape. Also, the engine has to be cranked over for it to work at all. To answer this problem, and to produce a more versatile tool than an ordinary compression tester, the "differential pressure gauge" was developed by aero engine techni-

cians during the 1940s. These instruments are now called "leak-down testers," or sometimes "cylinder leak testers."

The idea is to connect a source of compressed air to an engine cylinder, via the spark plug hole, and to measure the rate at which the air leaks past the seal of the rings and valves. (Obviously, the engine first has to be turned until the cylinder being tested has both its valves closed.) The compressed air comes from a shop's air line; the measurement of the leak is achieved by the leak-down tester.

The device consists of a pressure regulator, a pressure gauge, a calibrated orifice, plus a second pressure gauge, all connected together in series, in that order. (There are simpler versions that use just one gauge, but these are less satisfactory.) The tool is connected to the shop air supply, and the regulator adjusted to some arbitrary value, typically either 100 psi or 80 psi, as indicated by the first pressure gauge. Air then flows through the orifice (typically a 0.030-inch hole) and into the cylinder. If the cylinder is perfectly airtight, the pressure in the cylinder will rise until it matches the supply pressure, at which point the second pressure gauge, downstream of the orifice, will show exactly the same reading as the first.

Of course, all real-world engines leak at least a little, so air will bleed out of the cylinder at a rate that depends on the size of that leak, which can be thought of as a second orifice—bad rings equals a big hole; a tight cylinder equals a small one. Now, as long this "equivalent orifice" presents less resistance to flow than the orifice in the tool, the pressure between the two will not quite match the regulated pressure upstream. The difference in the readings of the two gauges thus gives a measure of the size of leak that exists.

Note that what the cylinder is leaking *into* is the atmosphere, so the actual reading on the downstream gauge will vary from place-to-place and from day-to-day, depending on altitude, barometric pressure, and other factors. While the aviation community deals with this problem by using a carefully calibrated master orifice (a sort of "dummy" leaking cylinder), and regulations set out in detail the manner in which the test is to be performed, there are no corresponding calibration standards for automotive leak-down testers. Nevertheless, one common practice is to adjust the regulator until the first

Leak-down testers, sometimes called cylinder leakage testers, or differential pressure testers, give a good picture of the state of an engine's valves and rings. The difference in reading between the two gauges indicates how fast air is leaking past those seals. This engine is mighty tight, with no visible difference between the two readings. *Karl Fredrickson photo, courtesy* Open Wheel *magazine*

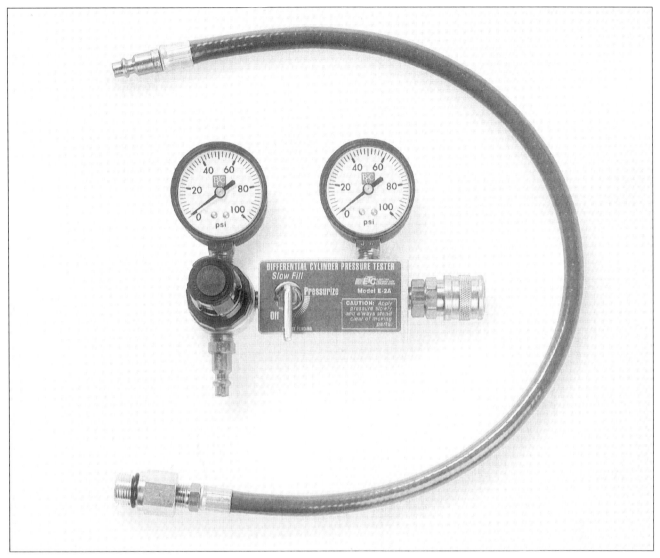

Leak-down testers were invented by the aviation industry; this model is the latest from that community and incorporates a "master orifice" that allows calibrating the instrument before use, to correct for altitude and local variations in atmospheric pressure. *Eastern Technology Corp.*

(upstream) pressure gauge reads 100 psi. The reading of the second gauge is then compared to that "100" reading. It is customary to express the difference between the two readings as a percentage; thus a reading of 90 psi on the second gauge would be termed "10 percent" leakage.

We might ask, "10 percent of *what*?" In fact, the 100-psi reference pressure is arbitrary; any other reasonable number might be used. In practice, and assuming a supply

regulated to 100 psi, a reading somewhere between 2 and 10 psi lower on the second gauge can be expected on a typical high-performance engine, the lower numbers suggesting an excellent valve job and a very tightly sealing ring assembly. (The test should be conducted on a warm/hot engine after shut-down, just like an ordinary compression check.)

A large amount of leakage from one cylinder may suggest a burned valve or other problem, but it may

also just be a valve held slightly off its seat by a piece of debris. To check for this, just lightly whack the valve end of the rocker with a plastic mallet; this will usually jar the grit loose. If not, the source of the leak can be tracked down by listening for air escaping at the engine intake, the exhaust pipe(s), and the crankcase breather/oil filler. Bubbles visible in the radiator header tank imply a leak at the head gasket. (Very small leaks—say 1 or 2 percent—can be inaudible.)

Air Density Meters

Every time an engine fills and empties its cylinders, a certain amount of air passes through it. To obtain the maximum power from that fixed quantity of air, a certain specific amount of fuel has to be provided, and it is the job of the carburetor(s) or fuel injection system to meter out that optimum amount of fuel. Trouble is, while the correct amount of fuel for a certain amount of air is a specific ratio by *weight*, carburetors and most fuel injection systems meter fuel according to the *volume* of air, not its weight. So the critical proportioning of fuel-to-air will be upset by any change in the relationship between the weight and the volume of air—by any change in air density, in other words.

Now, the density of air depends on several factors, but the major ones are temperature and barometric pressure. (It is also affected by humidity, but only to a

very slight extent.) At any constant pressure, cold air has a higher density than hot air—it is "thicker," if you like. Similarly, at any constant temperature, a pound of air at low pressure, as encountered at high altitudes, occupies more volume than that same pound of air at a higher pressure—it is "thinner." So, as all experienced engine tuners understand, to get maximum power from an air breathing engine, the amount of fuel supplied has to be adjusted to take account of both the temperature and the barometric pressure of the local atmosphere.

Now, you could measure barometric pressure with a barometer, and air temperature with a thermometer. This would give you almost all the basic data you need to establish local air density, but would necessitate some rather tedious mathematics to come up with a number relating those readings to a "standard atmosphere" of

59 degrees Fahrenheit and 29.92 inches of mercury (14.694 psi).

One tool that performs both measurements at once is an air density meter. It consists of a sealed metal bellows with a quantity of air trapped inside. One end of the bellows is linked to a pointer on the instrument's dial face, which gives a reading directly in percentage, with 100 percent corresponding to a standard atmosphere. Higher values indicate greater air density, whether from a lower temperature or a higher barometric pressure or both, and vice versa for lower readings.

Any drop in atmospheric pressure around the instrument allows the bellows to expand, moving the needle to a lower reading, and vice versa. Likewise, cooler air makes the air in the bellows shrink, moving the needle higher. Temperature compensation is thus built in and automatic. Just keep the instrument in the shade and allow it several minutes to adapt to changes.

Under any given set of conditions, there is only one fuel:air mixture setting that gives peak power. Carbs and most racing fuel injection systems cannot compensate for changes in air temperature or atmospheric pressure, however, so sharp tuners correct for these factors. One instrument that takes account of both at the same time is an air density meter. For convenience, these are calibrated directly in percentage of standard atmosphere density. *Kinsler Fuel Injection, Inc.*

C O N T E N T S

Volt/Ohm/Ammeters . . .102

Using a Multimeter 105

Measuring Temperature . 105

Liquid-in-Glass
Thermometers 105

Dial Thermometers 107

Pyrometers 107

Thermocouples 108

Noncontact Pyrometers . 111

Tachometers 113

Timing Lights 114

Measuring Volumes 116

Alignment Gauges
and Tools 118

Small, hand-held multimeters are fine for voltage and resistance (ohms) measurements, but inexpensive general-purpose ones cannot cope with the rather large currents (amperes) encountered in automotive electrical systems. Larger units for the bench-top, which *can*, are considerably more expensive. This one will handle up to 600 amps—enough to deal even with a husky starter motor.

MISCELLANEOUS MEASURING TOOLS

Volt/Ohm/Ammeters

To determine the electrical voltage or resistance between two points, a volt meter or ohm meter is needed. These two functions are often combined in one unit called a volt/ohmmeter (VOM) or "multimeter." An ammeter function is also usually included, but many ordinary multimeters are designed for use in electronics work, where currents are measured in milliamps—thousandths of an amp—and cannot handle the larger currents found in most automotive circuits. For automotive work, you want to be able to measure currents up to at least 10 amps; 30 would be better. Similar multimeters are available with a greatly expanded range of amperage scales, but ones with a capacity of even 10 amps are significantly more expensive.

The worst case is measuring the current draw of a starter motor, which can be as much as 500 amps. While ammeters are made that can cope with this, these Industrial Strength units are physically large and seriously expensive. The most practical alternative is an "inductive" ammeter, a device with a conventional gauge face, no visible wires, and something that looks like a broom clip on the back. This "U"-shaped bracket is simply slipped over the insulated cable carrying the starter current; the

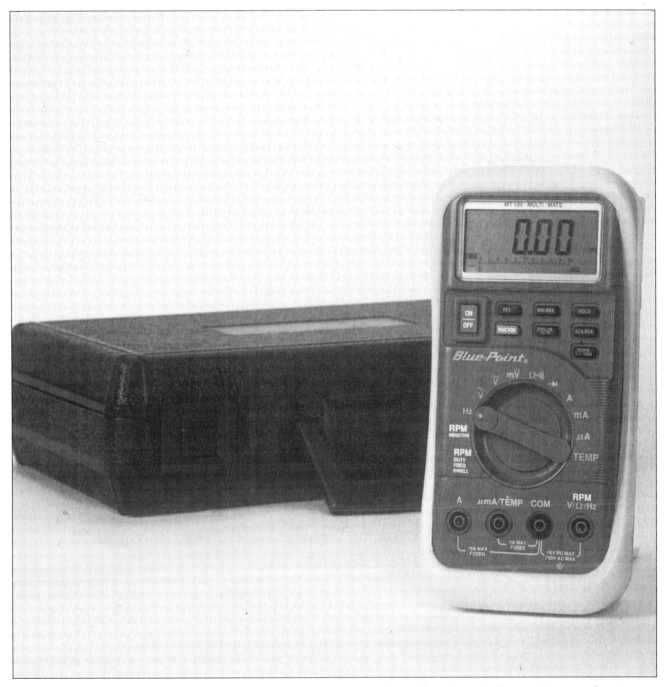

This hand-held digital multimeter is specifically designed for automotive work and, apart from the usual voltage and resistance functions, can measure currents up to 10 amps. That is many times the more typical fraction-of-an-amp limit of a general-purpose cheapie and is certainly helpful, but it is still not enough to measure, say, the output of an alternator. This unit also has numerous advanced functions, such as tach, frequency, pulse-width, etc. *Snap-on Tools Co.*

instrument measures the strength of the electromagnetic field around the conductor, and displays the result directly in amps.

Most of the cost of an ordinary VOM is in the meter itself, not the internal components. So, while a serviceable VOM can be had for as little as 10 bucks, for a bit more money you can get one with a meter face that is much larger, and therefore more readable. We are speaking here of an *analog* type of meter—the kind with a dial face and moving needle. There is also the option of a digital VOM, which simply shows a number on its display.

Most of the advantages of digital meters apply to electronics work, and are of little benefit in

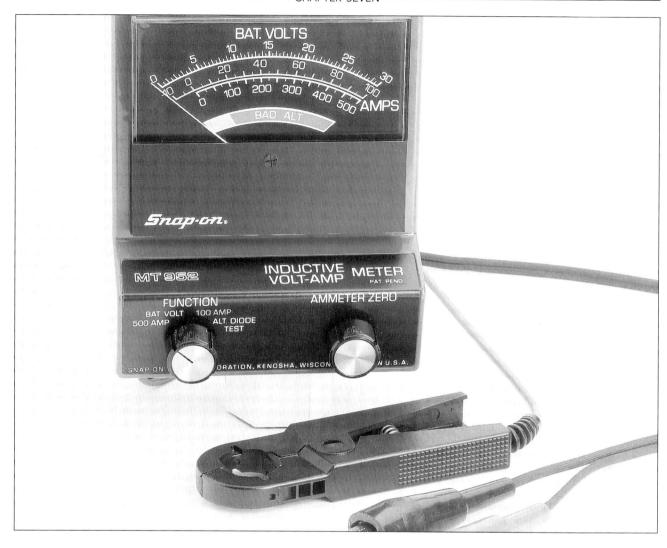

Large currents can be measured by an ammeter of practical size and cost by gauging the magnetic field around a conductor, rather than directly measuring the current flowing throughit. The clamp-like attachment on this volt-amp meter is simply clipped around the conductor, typically the starter cable. The meter displays the results direclty in amps.

automotive applications. (A digital VOM has an internal resistance many times greater than the analog type, which avoids affecting the tiny currents encountered in radios, TVs, computers, etc.) Any half-decent digital multimeter should have an accuracy of not worse than 1 percent on all scales; somewhat more expensive units claim better than 0.05 percent accuracy.

There are only two drawbacks to a digital VOM for general automotive work. First, they are more expensive; second, their internal circuitry requires a small amount of time to respond to a change. An analog meter is better at showing the kind of momentary variations that can occur when, for example, you wiggle a wire with an internal fracture. The needle on the analog meter will flick each time the circuit "makes" or "breaks." Under the same circumstances, a digital unit might never settle down to a readable number at all, or continue to show a constant value.

Because of the wide variety of applications in which these instruments are used, a VOM is equipped with a selector knob that allows adjusting the sensitivity of the meter, according to the size of the variable being measured. Separate scales on the meter face correspond to the different settings of the selector switch. A general-purpose VOM typically offers full-scale readings from 0.25 to 1,000 volts DC, and from 1 to 1,000 ohms.

While the voltage function obviously only returns useful information when the circuit is powered, a VOM must *never* be used to measure resistance on a "live" circuit. Not only will a false reading result, it is also highly likely that the meter will be irreparably damaged. A small battery within the meter makes it self-powered for resistance measurements. As this battery gradually weakens, the zero point on the scale (when in resistance mode) shifts; a thumb-wheel adjustment is provided to correct for this. You simply switch to resistance mode, "short" the two probes together, and turn the adjustment until it reads zero.

Using a Multimeter

When using a meter to establish what is going on in an automotive electrical circuit, there are four essential points to remember:

1. The voltage drop across a component is measured across the two terminals of the component; the meter is connected in parallel with the component;

2. The resistance within a component is likewise measured in parallel with the component;

3. Resistance should only ever be measured on an unpowered circuit; never connect an ohmmeter (including a VOM switched to an ohms scale) to a live circuit—you will surely fry the meter;

4. The current through a component is measured by placing the meter in series with the component—all the juice has to pass through the meter, which is why you can't use an inexpensive general-purpose VOM to measure, say, the output of a generator.

Measuring Temperature

Compared to most of the other physical quantities discussed in this book, temperature is a somewhat fuzzy thing. While there is a theoretical basis for a temperature "standard," there is no standardized "degree" inside a glass case in some national bureau of standards. For practical purposes, temperatures are based on secondary standards, often the freezing or melting points of pure substances.

Liquid-in-Glass Thermometers

The cheapest, simplest, and most familiar type of thermometer consists of a slim glass tube with a very tiny bore down its center and a bulb-shaped reservoir at the bottom. The bulb holds a store of a liquid, usually mercury; within the working range of the instrument, the liquid also extends part way up the central bore, or *capillary*.

It is generally supposed that the mercury expands when heated and so rises in the capillary, but in fact *both* the mercury *and* the glass tube expand, though at different rates. This is not mere academic quibbling; this has a bearing on how a mercury thermometer must be used in order to achieve an accurate measurement. (Otherwise, about the only precaution needed is the obvious one—don't break it.)

There is no problem when measuring, say, local air temperature, because the glass and the mercury column are both exposed to the same temperature over their full length. However, when the thermometer is partly immersed in a fluid that is hotter or cooler than the surrounding air, the portion of the capillary tube and the mercury column that extend up into the air will not be at the same temperature as the "working" end, and the difference in their expansions will potentially sabotage the accuracy of the reading. Accordingly, any decent lab or industrial mercury thermometer will come with a specification as to how deep the instrument should be immersed. This also means that mercury thermometers are not really suitable for measuring the temperature of the surface of a solid. That does not mean, however, that they are not affected by the temperature of surfaces they contact. Ideally, a mercury thermometer should not contact anything other than the fluid it is gauging; to this end, some come with an eye formed at the top, for hanging.

Because mercury freezes at about -38 degrees Fahrenheit, a different liquid—alcohol or toluene—is used for thermometers that measure below that point. At normal atmospheric pressure, mercury boils at 357.3 degrees Celsius (675.14 degrees Fahrenheit), so conventional mercury-in-glass thermometers are limited to the range between these two end-points. The upper end of the range can be extended to about 600 degrees Celsius (about 1,100 degrees Fahrenheit) by filling the space above the mercury column with a pressurized gas, often nitrogen.

As is common with measuring tools, there is a trade-off between range, precision, and size. While there are both Fahrenheit and Celsius versions of mercury thermometers with an overall length of about 16 inches that span from -10 to 400 degrees C, or 14 to 752 degrees F (the high end being extended by slight pressurizing), these have rather coarse divisions, typically 2 degrees C, or 5 degrees F. Precision mercury thermometers of about the same length that read in divisions of 0.1 Celsius degrees or 0.2 Fahrenheit degrees have a much narrower range; it takes six such instruments to span from -38 to 155 C, or -36 to 311 F. Broad-range, low-precision items are dirt cheap—say $5–$10; even the high

precision units are generally well under $100.

Because of the near impossibility of making the capillary bore exactly uniform throughout its length, the limit of accuracy for any mercury thermometer is about 0.5 degrees F (0.3 degrees C). While "reference standard" mercury thermometers can be had, the only difference between these several hundred dollar devices and an "ordinary" $50 precision thermometer is a set of tables supplied with the unit that gives the corrections, based on careful lab calibration, at a handful of specific reference points, accurate to 0.005 degrees C.

While not as cheap as standard mercury thermometers, dial-type thermometers are not expensive. Because you can only squeeze so many markings onto a dial face, there is a trade-off between range and precision. Within the limits of readability, accuracy can be 1 percent or better. Probe-equipped ones are intended for immersion in a liquid or gas; there are also surface-mount models. *Copyright Omega Engineering, Inc. Reproduced courtesy of Omega Engineering, Inc., Stamford, CT 06907*

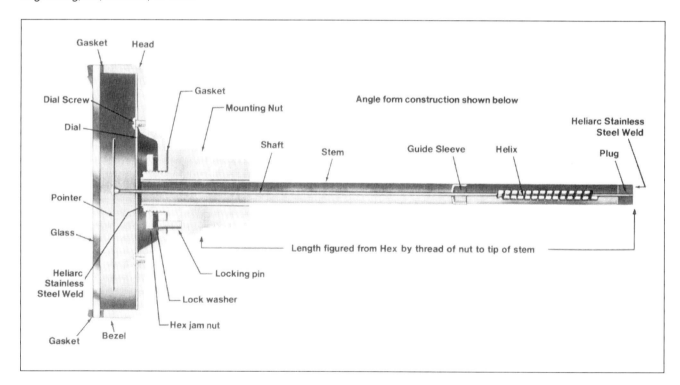

As in most dial thermometers, the working element in this probe-type unit is a bimetal strip that curls and uncurls with changes in temperature. Here, the strip is wound into a helix, or spiral. This gives the free end of the strip sufficient movement so no amplifying gear train is needed—the end of the strip is simply connected to the pointer shaft. *Copyright Omega Engineering, Inc. Reproduced courtesy of Omega Engineering ,Inc., Stamford, CT 06907*

Dial Thermometers

The next most common type of thermometer is the mechanical dial type. For their working element these use a bimetallic strip—two ribbons of different metals fused together back-to-back. On heating, the two metals expand at different rates and so cause the strip to curl. To amplify the resulting movement, the strip is made long and wound into a flat spiral, like a clock-spring, or into a helix, like the stripe on a barber's pole. A pointer attached to the free end of the bimetallic strip accordingly moves, indicating the temperature on a dial face. Dial type-thermometers are much more rugged than the mercury-in-glass ones, and are much easier to read.

This principle applies to many kinds of thermometers, from industrial instruments to the ordinary household meat thermometer. (A motorcycle racing friend determined that a safe oil temperature was somewhere between "Roast Beef" and "Turkey." No kidding.) Despite their simplicity and low cost, these devices can be surprisingly accurate; one common industrial brand claims an accuracy of ± 1 percent of full scale.

They come in two types: Those for surface temperature measurement and those having a probe for immersion into a fluid. Dial faces for the probe type run from about 1 1/2 inches to 5 inches diameter; stem lengths from 2 1/2 to 36 inches, but 9 inches is most common. While some combinations of fluid and temperature will give an accurate reading with just 2 inches immersion, 5 inches will keep you on the safe side at any temperature in any kind of fluid.

The familiar problem of scale size vs. precision vs. range emerges

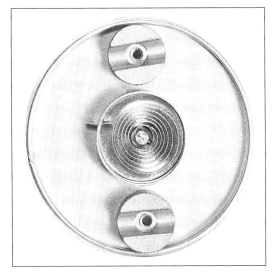

This surface temperature measuring dial thermometer has its bimetal strip wound into a flat coil, like a clock spring. As in the previous picture, the strip is long enough that it can drive the pointer directly, making for a dead-simple and trouble-free unit. Contrast this with the arrangement in the previous picture. The magnets secure the instrument to any iron-based surface. *Copyright Omega Engineering, Inc. Reproduced courtesy of Omega Engineering, Inc., Stamford, CT 06907*

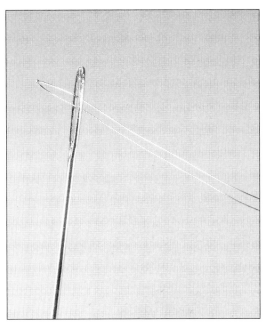

A thermocouple is simply two wires, made of different metals, joined together. The wires can be of any size, but size affects the time it takes to respond to a temperature change. These very fine thermocouple wires will have virtually no measurable time lag, but are very fragile and, simply because of their small size, will corrode rapidly in a harsh environment. *Copyright Omega Engineering, Inc. Reproduced courtesy of Omega Engineering, Inc., Stamford, CT 06907*

here, too. While there are wide-range units spanning from -50 to 300 F, or 150-750 F, or 200 to 1,000 F (and corresponding Celsius versions), these have divisions 10 Fahrenheit (or 5 Celsius) degrees apart. Resolution of 1 or 2 degrees is available only over a much narrower range. (And bear in mind that the accuracy is expressed as a percentage of full scale; you do not want to trust one of these things working near the bottom of its range. Select accordingly.)

Pyrometers

By the most general definition, pyrometers and thermometers are the same thing—both measure temperature. A distinction made in general usage, though, is that thermometers measure comparatively low temperatures, while pyrometers measure high ones. Five hundred degrees F is sometimes suggested as the break-point, but many devices classed as pyrometers can also measure down to room temperature or below.

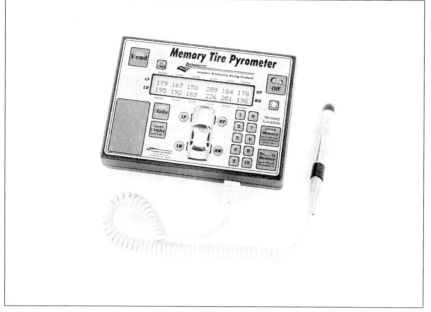

Tires cool off rapidly once the car is stopped, so a tire pyrometer needs to have rapid response to get useful measurements. This one has the advantage of a display that simultaneously shows three values—inside edge, outside edge, and center—for each of four tires, plus a memory that can store up to 10 such 12-point values. *Longacre Automotive Racing Products*

Apart from some limitations on the highest temperatures they can operate at, liquid-in-glass and dial-type thermometers have the drawback that they are not "remote reading"—you have to be quite near the hot stuff to read the instrument.

Thermocouples

While there are other means to measure temperatures at a distance, about the most popular way in industry and in automotive engineering is through the use of *thermocouples*. In 1821, the German physicist J.T. Seebeck discovered that when two wires made of different metals are joined together at both ends, a small electrical current will flow around the loop whenever the two junction points are at different temperatures. By measuring the voltage across the loop, the temperature difference between the two junctions can be established.

This *thermoelectric effect*, as it is called, appears with every combination of two different metals, but some pairs work better than others. Materials that grow excessively brittle or corrode rapidly at high temperatures are obviously unsuitable. Further, while the actual voltage developed by any metal-pair combination is very small, and so comparatively difficult to measure, some put out more "juice" than others. Also, some of the potential metals, such as platinum, that comfortably tolerate high temperatures are rare and accordingly expensive. As a result, a handful of specific combinations have become standardized for thermocouple applications. Of this handful, three are commonplace, identified as types "J," "K," and "T."

Type "J" thermocouples use iron for one wire and a copper-nickel alloy called *constantan* for the other. These materials are relatively inexpensive, and so are popular for applications within their range—about 0 F to 1,400 F. Type "K" thermocouples use a combination of *chromel*—a nickel-chromium alloy—and *alumel*—a nickel-aluminum alloy. While somewhat more expensive than type "K" thermocouples, the chromel/alumel combination extends the upper temperature limit to 2,000–2,300

Temperature Calibration Points

	Fahrenheit	Celsius
Freezing point of mercury	-38	-38.9
Ice point	32	0
Boiling point of water	212	100
Freezing point of tin	449.4	231.9
Freezing point of lead	621.5	327.5
Boiling point of sulfur	832.4	444.7
Freezing point of aluminum	1220.7	660.4

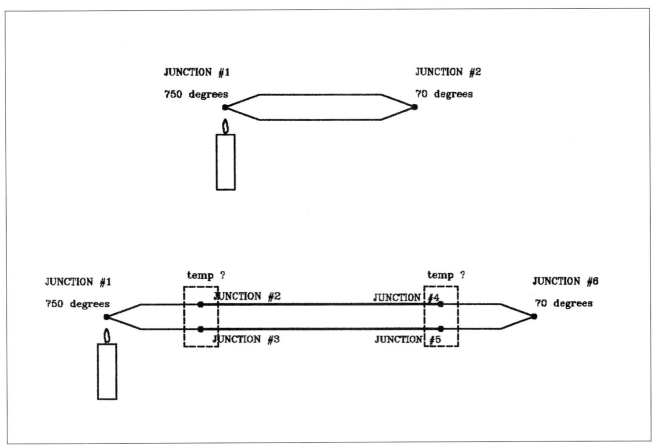

JUNCTION #1

750 degrees

JUNCTION #2

70 degrees

JUNCTION #1

750 degrees

temp ?

JUNCTION #2

JUNCTION #3

temp ?

JUNCTION #4

JUNCTION #5

JUNCTION #6

70 degrees

A thermocouple-based pyrometer (top) does not directly measure temperature, but rather measures the temperature *difference* between two points, a "hot" junction and a reference, or "cold" junction. Adding extension wires to stretch the reach of a thermocouple (bottom) introduces *four* additional junctions. While the temperature at junctions No. 4 and No. 5 may be very close to that at junction No. 6, where the meter is, it is very hard to avoid effects from junctions No. 2 and No. 3. Always use purpose-made extension wires, never plain copper.

F, and is more corrosion resistant. Type "T" thermocouples use constantan for one wire and pure copper for the other. They are low in cost, yet tend to be more accurate than most others up to about 300 F, but are limited to about 700 F. One or another of these three is the basis for most all contact-type pyrometers sold for automotive instrumentation.

It is vital to bear in mind that a thermocouple does not directly gauge temperature. What it does is gauge the temperature *difference* between two points . . . that at the measuring or "hot" junction, and that at the reference or "cold" junction. Thus, before the electrical

output of a thermocouple can be used to determine the temperature of the "hot" junction, the temperature of the "cold" junction has to be known.

The need to have a second "thermometer" in order for your first "thermometer" to be of any use is, to say the least, inconvenient. Accordingly, in thermocouple-based pyrometers, the cold junction is located within the instrument and some sort of internal electronic compensation for the cold junction temperature is built-in. Also built-in is a set of corrections to take account of the fact that the output of a thermocouple is nonlinear—successive equal rises

in temperature cause slightly *un*equal increases in the output. The difficulty of making an analog (needle-and-dial) type of meter that can accurately measure such a small voltage means that most pyrometers now on the market use a digital display. These are sold for measuring the temperatures of tires, race-track surfaces, exhaust gases, various engine parts, coolant, oil, etc.

The accuracy of a thermocouple-based instrument cannot be higher than that of the wire itself. The American National Standards Institute (ANSI) has proposed standards for the accuracy of thermocouple wire. For types "J" and

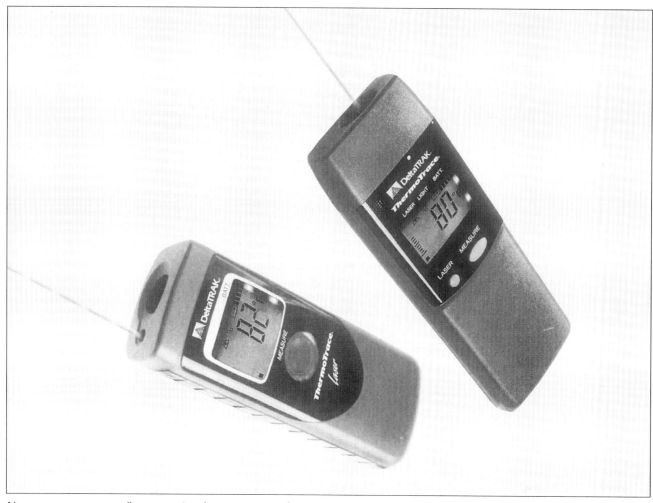

Noncontact pyrometers allow measuring the temperature of moving surfaces. These devices take the average temperature over an *area* rather than at a point and, like the beam from a flashlight, the area covered depends on the distance from the surface. Some premium units have a laser that points to the middle of the "spot," but that tells nothing about its size, which may include cooler or hotter areas. *Argo Manufacturing Co.*

"K," the limits are plus-or-minus 2.2 C, or 0.75 percent, *whichever is greater*. While premium grade wire is available that cuts these permissible error margins roughly in half, there seems reason to be skeptical of claims by some digital thermometer suppliers of accuracies of ± 1 degree between 0 and, say, 1,400 degrees F. (An error of 0.75 percent of 1,400 degrees is a bit more than 10 degrees.)

For our purposes, only exhaust gas temperature meters will be operating that hot, and the readings obtained are essentially used for comparative purposes anyway.

So, in truth, a high degree of absolute accuracy is not necessary. Given the "plug-in-and-go" nature of these packaged products, about all the user need do is to ensure that he does not introduce any further errors because of the installation.

One guaranteed way to get hopelessly inaccurate readings from a thermocouple-based instrument is to plug in the wrong type of thermocouple—the internal cold junction compensation and the correction curves will only be appropriate for one type. To reduce confusion, the connecting plugs on store-bought thermocouples are

color coded. Another trouble area is extension wire. While most thermocouple wire is not extremely expensive, it is not dirt-cheap either, so it is tempting to use only a small amount of it and to extend the leads to the instrument using something cheaper. And here lies a problem.

From the above description of the operating principle of a thermocouple, it should be obvious that extending a thermocouple by splicing in two lengths of, say, copper wire introduces four new junctions, and each of these will also operate as a thermocouple. For accuracy, then, only specially calibrated thermocouple extension wire should be used, of a type appropriate to the nature of the thermocouple. Also, the primary thermocouple wires should be long enough that the connection to the extension wires comes at a place that is near the same temperature as the meter containing the reference junction.

Bear in mind, too, that anything that changes the metallurgy of thermocouple wire will also alter its thermoelectric properties. Excessive stretching or bending of the wires should be avoided during installation, and the effect of exposure to harsh environments on the chemistry of the metals needs to be checked occasionally. Calibration can be checked by using the known melting or boiling points of various substances. Some useful reference temperatures are given in the accompanying table.

A suitable insulation/sheathing needs to be provided to protect the thermocouple wire from mechanical damage and from heat (except for the small area around the hot junction, of course), but another factor that needs to be guarded against is electrical interference. The tiny voltage developed by the thermocouple is easily swamped by the electrical "noise" of an automobile's ignition system. A grounded flexible metal sheath, like BX cable, is used to shield the wires against this radio frequency (RF) interference.

To protect the hot junction from physical damage and oxidation, it is often enclosed in a protective sheath. This is the outside of the "probe" frequently supplied with store-bought units. This slows down the response of the thermocouple, however, so when a fleeting peak temperature needs to be

gauged, the thermocouple is used "bare," even if at the expense of its service life. Bare-wire thermocouples can be welded to washers, such as under spark plugs, or buried in small drillings in brake pads, in which case it is secured in place with something called Sauriesen cement. . . . The applications are limited only by the imagination.

Noncontact Pyrometers

The types of thermometers/pyrometers we have discussed so far all need to be in contact with the hot stuff in order to work. Sometimes, however, making contact is inconvenient or impossible, such as when the hot object is moving. One of several methods of measuring the temperature of an object without touching it is *infrared* (IR) *pyrometry*.

To explain, all objects at a temperature above absolute zero emit electromagnetic radiation. It turns out that, while hot objects emit radiation over a *range* of wavelengths, most of it appears at some specific wavelength, according to the temperature of the object. At high temperatures we can see some of this radiation in the form of light of a certain color (hence "red-hot" and "white-hot"), because the radiation has a wavelength that is within the range our eyes can detect. At lower temperatures, we can still *feel* the radiation as heat even though we can no longer see it—its wavelength has grown too long for our eyes (but not for our skin) to sense. Infrared pyrometers are instruments that can "see" this longer wavelength radiation.

Once rare and expensive, IR pyrometers now start at under $200 and are growing in popularity. Obvious automotive applications include taking the temperature of rotating tires and brake rotors; here

no conventional thermometer could be used. But noncontact pyrometers can also show advantages in some situations where others might compete. While other thermometers measure only at some small, localized point, an IR pyrometer averages the reading over an area—a small circular "spot." This has advantages where a point-measuring thermometer, such as a thermocouple, might return a figure that, while accurate, is nevertheless misleading because it happens to be located at a particularly hot or particularly cool spot. This averaging characteristic also has its drawbacks: If the unit is aimed from a distance of several feet at, say, a radiator, the spot may be so large that it is including part of the fender or hood. To aid in aiming, some "deluxe" models have a laser pointer that marks the center of the spot . . . but it does *not* indicate its size.

By design, the detecting lens of an IR pyrometer has a field of view that extends over some small angle, so the size of circular spot that it "sees" depends on the distance of the instrument from the surface it is measuring. For typical automotive aftermarket units, the diameter of the spot is about 1/8 the distance to the surface. Thus, at a distance of 6 inches, the spot would be about 3/4 inch in diameter; at 36 inches, about 8 1/2 inches, and so on. The devices are useful out to about 10 feet.

Depending on make, model, and price, the range of an IR pyrometer is from about -25 F (-32 C) to around 750–900 F (400–482 C) or to 1,600 F (870 C), although the higher temperature units are about twice the price. Theoretically, the potential accuracy of these devices can approach plus-or-

Exhaust gas temperature is a key indicator of mixture strength and thus a valuable engine tuning aid. While there is no "correct" value, once experience with a particular engine is gained, the effect of changes in mixture strength, spark advance, compression ratio, fuel quality, and other variables will be reflected. Also, variations between individual cylinders will reveal mixture distribution problems. *Doug Gore photo, courtesy* Stock Car Racing *magazine*

minus 0.5 percent, but 1–2 percent is probably more realistic. In this connection, it is noteworthy that at least one IR pyrometer offered to the automotive aftermarket resolves down to 0.1 degree. Since this instrument reads to 750 F, and since even 0.5 percent of 750 is 3.75, it is reasonable to ask if this resolution is justifiable. So we asked.

It turns out that while the *accuracy* is ± 2 degrees—that is, a surface at 325 might actually read as anywhere between 323 and 327—the *repeatability* is good enough that useful information can be had from a finer resolution. Thus, if the difference in measured temperature between the edge and the center of a tire is 3.5 degrees, it can be assumed with confidence that, while the absolute number displayed may be out by 1 or 2 degrees, the actual temperature difference is in fact 3.5 degrees, ± 0.1.

Tachometers

In the mechanical speedometers and tachometers once universal in cars, the working principle is the "eddy current." A small bar magnet, driven directly by the speedo/tach cable, spins around inside a close-fitting shallow drum; the pull of the rotating magnet, which increases with speed, tends to drag the drum around with it. The movement of the drum, though, is restrained by a spiral clock spring, so the drum will turn only until the spring force matches the magnetic force. The drum, in turn, is directly connected to the pointer that indicates the speed or rpm on the instrument face.

Eddy current devices are cheap, but are prone to errors from a variety of causes, including a gradual loss of magnetism, a progressive weakening of the spring, plus temperature sensitivity and all

the manufacturing variables affecting the linearity of that spring's rate. Some idea of the vagueness of a mass-production eddy current instrument for speed measuring is revealed by the speedometer errors of more than 1,000 production cars. A total of 38.5 percent of the vehicles had speedos in error by 5 percent or more at an indicated 60 miles per hour; 6.5 percent were off by more than 10 percent. Modern electronic instruments for measuring rotational speed do much better than that.

The earliest type of "electronic" tachometer involved a precision DC generator driven from somewhere on the rotating machinery. With increasing speed, the generator put out more volts, and that voltage was measured by a voltmeter, with its face calibrated in rpm. Although still used in some specialized applications, this and other previous methods have been largely overtaken by more modern electronics.

Modern electronic tachometers—both analog and digital, whether hand-held, in-dash, or bench-mounted—involve a pulse generator of some sort, circuitry that converts the frequency of the pulses into a variable voltage, plus an indicating meter that again amounts to a voltmeter calibrated in rpm. The pulses may come from a rotating magnet that sweeps past a sensing head, from flashes of light reflected by a shiny patch on some rotating part or, as is often the case with engines, from the ignition system.

Bench-type tach/dwell meters from automotive tool suppliers are usually triggered by an inductive pickup that reads the electromagnetic pulses from an engine's ignition system. (The "dwell" function doesn't have much application in these days of electronic ignition

systems. It displays the number of crankshaft degrees during which the ignition points are closed, by measuring other aspects of these pulses.) These are generally analog meter (needle-and-dial) instruments with a range of 0–10,000 rpm, and a resolution of either 10 or 20 rpm; best accuracy, then, cannot be better than 1 percent. Digital instruments for general industrial use resolve down to 1 rpm and claim accuracies as high as ± 0.02 percent of the indicated value. These may be magnetically or optically (flash-of-light) triggered; some will accept either type of input. Others have a protruding shaft with a tapered rubber point that can be poked onto or into the end of a rotating shaft.

The most accurate way to gauge rotational speed, and a method used to calibrate other tachometers, is with a *stroboscope*. Here, a flashing light is used to illuminate some rotating part of a machine. The flashes, generated by a Xenon flash tube, are extremely brief, so the effect is to "freeze" the movement of the rotating part when the flashes come exactly one revolution apart. The timing of the flashes can be adjusted by a control knob on the scope, and that frequency displayed on a (usually) digital meter.

Apart from the potential for a very slight reading error (is it truly "frozen," or is it creeping very slowly forward or back?), the accuracy of this form of tachometry depends only on the internal "clock" that times the flashes. How accurate is that clock? Well, if you recall from Chapter 1, my office digital clock implies a precision of better than 99.9988 percent. As for accuracy, as I write now, several months later, that clock is still 2 minutes slow. By rough estimate,

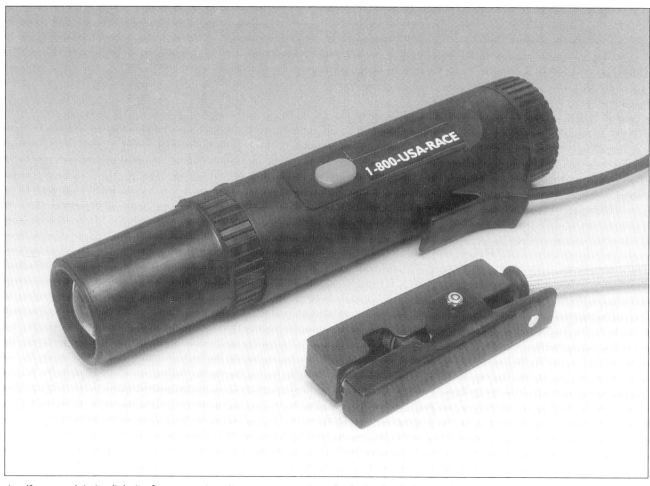

A self-powered timing light is often convenient. For magneto-equipped vehicles that lack an on-board battery, they are essential. This one uses an inductive pickup that clips around the No. 1 plug lead, and works to 10,000 rpm. *Powerhouse Products*

that $10 throwaway item is accurate to at least 1 part in 8,000,000! You can expect a stroboscope to at least match that.

About the only caution regarding the use of a stroboscope is the potential for "multiple" and "submultiple" errors. A shaft rotating at 1,200 rpm (20 revolutions per second) will appear frozen by a flash occurring 20 times per second, but it will also appear frozen at a flash rate of 10 revolutions per second, or 40 revolutions per second. Usually, though, rpm can be guestimated to within plus-or-minus 50 percent, so in practice this is not quite as big a problem as it seems. On the other hand, if the

object being illuminated is not, say, a pulley with a mark on it but rather, for example, a gear with 40 teeth, then there are a great many different flash rates that will "freeze" the gear teeth. A single identifying mark (the part number, a chalk mark) is needed to avoid wholesale confusion.

Timing Lights

If you think the above description of a stroboscope sounds a lot like a timing light, you're right. A timing light is nothing but a stroboscope that is triggered not by an internal clock but rather by an inductive pickup that reads the pulse of electricity

flowing through the plug wire when the No. 1 cylinder fires. The light, when shone on the timing marks engraved into the front pulley or vibration damper, will freeze the motion, allowing gauging of the amount of ignition advance by viewing which timing mark appears stationary next to a fixed pointer.

While many timing lights obtain their power from the vehicle, others are self-powered by an internal battery. When a vehicle, such as a magneto-equipped race car, has no on-board battery, this is a necessity. Most timing lights are good to 10,000 rpm, which may seem like overkill, since most

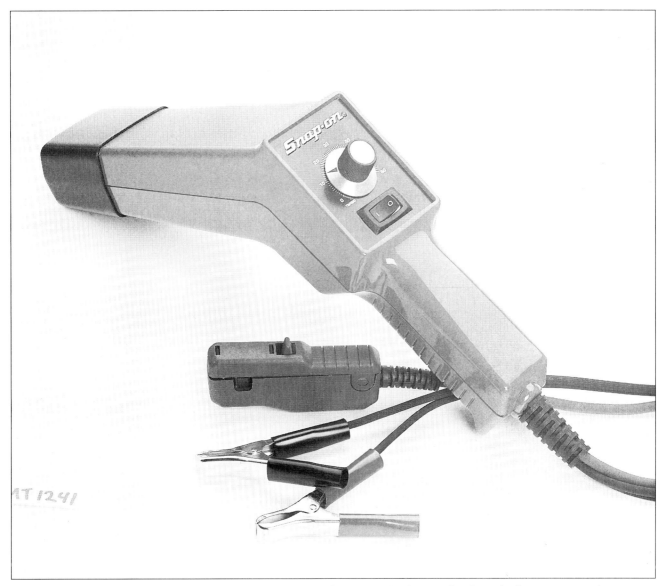

"Dial-back" timing lights flash *before* the spark occurs by a number of degrees set by the user. This allows checking an ignition advance curve when only a single factory timing mark is stamped on the front pulley or vibration damper. The "anticipation" of the tool, however, is calculated based on the time between the previous two sparks; a "lumpy" idle will upset this calculation. Also, few if any of these devices will work with a multiple spark discharge ignition system. *Snap-on Tools Co.*

street engines have their ignition fully advanced by 4,000 rpm or so. However, some race engines have advance curves that keep going to 8,000 rpm and beyond (and some folks actually stick their head in there to use a timing light with the engine turning that fast! Not me, thanks).

While a front pulley or vibration damper with degree marks all around its circumference can be used with any timing light, many production engines have a much smaller range of marks, and sometimes just a single one. In these cases, a "dial-back" or "timing/advance" light is needed if any variation from the single factory timing is to be gauged. These employ an internal clock chip that causes the flash to occur some adjustable number of degrees "before" the actual firing of the plug. (It is not really

"anticipating" the next firing; it is actually measuring the time since the last one.) While useful under some circumstances, the internal tachometer function that judges when the next ignition jolt should arrive based on the time between the previous two can be confused by the constant speed variations of a "lumpy" idle. This will cause the timing to appear to wander even though it is actually unchanging.

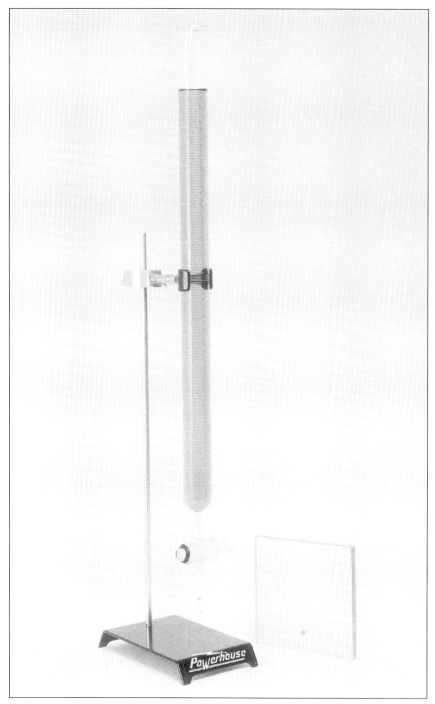

A burette is simply a graduated column with a spigot on the bottom. By comparing the amount of fluid in the burette before and after fluid is dispensed to fill a space, the volume of that space is measured. The most common automotive application is in "CC-ing" combustion chambers. The square of plastic is used to close off the top of the cylinder head; the fluid is dispensed through the hole in the plate. *Powerhouse Products*

Another thing to watch for is multiple spark discharge ignition systems. Here, sparks do not occur as single, isolated events, but rather as a constant series of sparks. This will confuse a "dial-back" type of timing light. Indeed, they may upset some fixed types too. Inquire before buying.

Measuring Volumes

We work with volume measurements all the time—a quart of this, a gallon of that—yet high accuracy in these units of measurement is seldom needed. That is a good thing, because it is also quite difficult to achieve.

The dimensions of regularly shaped solids—a sphere, a rectangular lump—can be measured, and their volumes calculated. Irregular ones, however, are a bitch. Two practical ways of establishing the volume of an odd-shaped solid are to weigh it, then calculate the volume based on the known density of the material it is made from, or to sink it into a fluid and gauge the volume of fluid it displaces. (Even when measuring fluids, when high accuracy is an issue, it is often preferable to determine the volume by calculation based on weight.)

Direct gauging of a fluid volume can be achieved with a graduated beaker—really just a glorified kitchen measuring cup. Bearing in mind the familiar problem of range vs. size vs. resolution, it is easy to understand why accuracy is improved if the container is made tall and thin, rather than short and squat. Graduated cylinders have the appropriate shape and are available in both plastic and glass, with capacities from 10 ml (10 milliliters . . . a milliliter is 1/1,000 of a liter) to 4,000 ml. In the sizes spanning 50–250 ml, graduations are at 1- or 2-ml intervals; plastic ones

Fixed-installation alignment rigs are the last word in precision measurement of wheel angles, but they are absurdly expensive and are most definitely not portable. Most folks who do their own alignment, especially on race cars, use more old-fashioned tools. This caster/camber gauge clamps magnetically to the hub and reads out positive or negative camber on the two outboard bubble tubes; caster is read off the center one (see text). *Longacre Automotive Racing Products*

run $10–20, glass ones twice that. Larger sizes are more coarsely graduated—5-ml divisions are usual on the 500-ml size, for example. Graduated cylinders are calibrated for 20 C (68 F); accuracy is better than one division. Ensure the cylinder is plumb, and align your eye with the fluid surface to avoid parallax error.

A volume measuring tool more commonly associated with automotive work is the *burette*—essentially a graduated cylinder with a tap on the bottom. These are used when "CC-ing" a combustion chamber—measuring its volume. The burette is set up plumb in a holder and filled with some arbitrary amount of fluid, and a read-

ing taken of this base-line amount. The fluid can be water with a few drops of food coloring and a drop or two of dishwashing detergent, to reduce the surface tension and so the meniscus curves. A 50-50 water-methanol mixture is sometimes recommended.

Meanwhile, the combustion chamber to be measured is arranged beneath the spigot on the burette so that the head deck surface is perfectly horizontal. With valves and spark plug in place, a small rectangle of Plexiglas™ with a finger-sized hole in it is set over the combustion chamber, and sealed to the head deck with a smear of grease. The tap on the

burette is then carefully opened and fluid allowed to dribble into the combustion chamber through the hole in the plastic, until the fluid rises to completely fill the chamber. A second reading is now taken from the burette and the amount of fluid delivered, and so the chamber volume is simply the base-line figure minus this one.

Note that the true combustion chamber volume is not just the volume of the cavity in the head; account also has to be taken of the free volume in the cylinder above the piston at TDC. In the case of flat-top pistons, this can be done by measurement and calculation, but pistons with domes or valve

Adapters to jig a bubble-type caster camber/gauge against the wheel rim, rather than the hub or spindle, add convenience, but accuracy now depends on the straightness of the rims. *Longacre Automotive Racing Products*

cut-outs can cause some head scratching. The burette technique can be used to measure this volume, too. Again, a smear of grease is necessary to seal the rings. If a piston dome extends above the block deck, a useful trick is to move the piston some known distance, say exactly 1/2 inch (use a dial gauge), perform the measurement, then calculate the volume of a cylinder with the applicable bore and a length of 1/2 inch, and subtract that from the measured volume.

With a burette and a depth gauge, it is simple to calculate how much to have machined off a cylinder head to raise the compression ratio to some specific new value. After determining the present chamber volume, calculate the desired chamber volume. Then, with the head jigged as before, dispense just exactly that new amount into the empty chamber. The distance from the fluid level to the deck is the amount that has to come off.

Alignment Gauges and Tools

Most of the precision measuring instruments we have dealt with in this book are general-purpose tools that would be just as useful for, say, constructing a home-built aircraft, or making some specialized tools or jigs for machine shop use, as for automotive work. We turn now to some automotive-specific tools designed for measuring the orientation of an automobile's wheels—alignment tools, in short.

Digital caster/camber gauges claim 10 times the precision of the conventional bubble type, reading to 0.1 degree. A tenfold increase in precision, and accuracy that is claimed to justify that fine resolution, for a twofold price increase seems like a bargain. *Intercomp Co.*

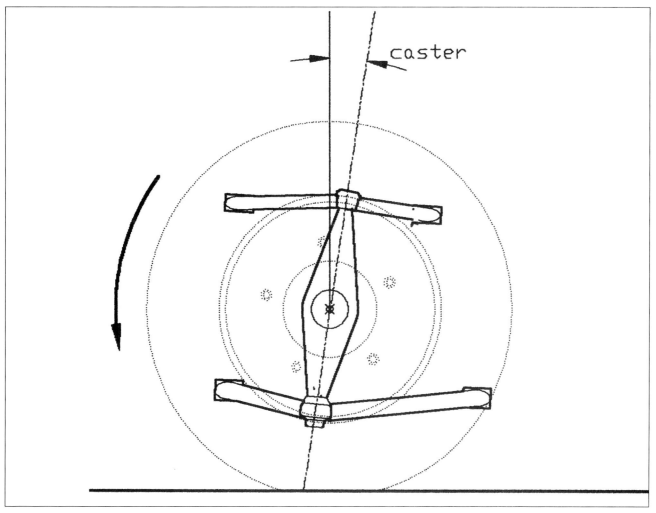

caster

Caster is the inclination of the steering swivel axis, relative to a true vertical. A modest amount of positive caster, as shown here, gives a vehicle's steering a degree of self-centering, because the tire trails behind the point on the road where the steering axis intersects.

The major dimensions we are concerned with here are *camber*, *caster*, and *toe-in* (or toe-out).

Camber is the side-to-side inclination of a wheel. Most road cars have camber angles between perhaps a degree or so negative (i.e., a pair of wheels closer together at the top), to some fraction of a degree positive. Most race cars have a fair bit of negative camber. The tool most often used to gauge this setting amounts to a spirit (bubble) level, secured to a fixture that mounts to the wheel or hub. This mounting is often magnetic; adapters of various sorts are avail-

able to permit gauging off the rim edges, rather than the wheel center. The variation of the spindle axis from the true horizon is the camber angle, indicated directly in degrees by engraved markings on the vial.

Commercially available bubble-type camber gauges span a range of about 6 degrees both ways, typically with a resolution of 1/4 degree. With care (see also the section on levels in Chapter 5), the gauge can be read to about twice that degree of precision. Recently, digital camber gauges have become available with a precision of 0.1 degree. These claim accuracy up to

10 times greater than traditional bubble gauges. In these instruments is a vial containing an electrolyte with three electrodes protruding down into the fluid. The center electrode is "live"; the other two are detectors. A tilt in the electrolyte level will accordingly change the resistance between the center electrode and each of the other two, a difference easily converted into a numerical display.

Whatever the type of gauge, for accuracy the vehicle must be on a level surface. A 1/2 degree tilt to the left, for example, will automatically add an error of 1/2 degree of

It is more difficult to obtain an accurate measure of caster than of camber, in part because gauging the caster requires steering the wheel a set number of degrees (usually 20), first to one side, then to the other, and the success of the whole operation depends on the accuracy of this movement. Greater precision here is possible using "Lazy-Susan" wheel platforms, called turn plates, that are marked directly in degrees. *Longacre Automotive Racing Products*

While unnecessary for ordinary caster measurements, digital turn plates have fine enough resolution (0.1 degree) that they also make it possible to establish the mis-match between left and right front wheel steer angles that result from Ackerman effects. *Intercomp Co.*

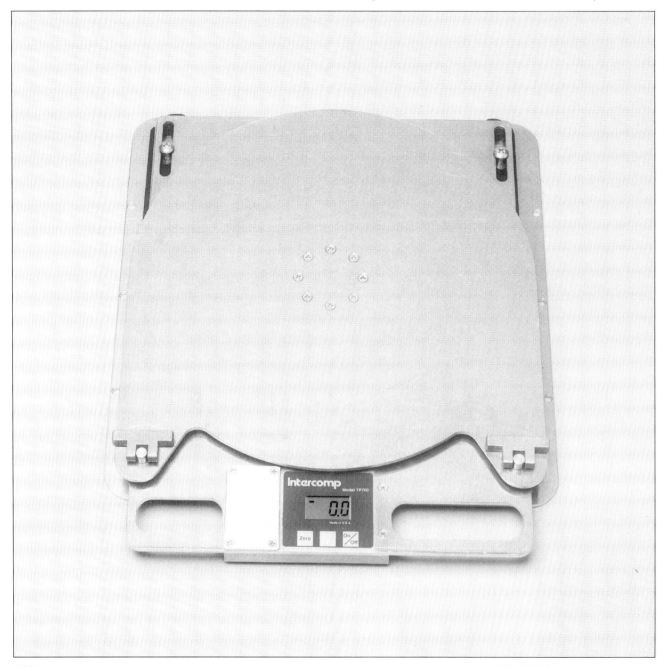

negative camber to the right side wheel(s) and 1/2 degree of positive to the right. Also, the tool must be oriented so it lies truly horizontal in a fore-and-aft plane—that is, the case must not tilt up or down toward the front or back of the car. A supplementary bubble is provided to aid this initial setup.

If a vehicle is viewed from the side, an imaginary line drawn through the top and bottom ball-joints of the front suspension will not usually be perfectly vertical; generally, the line will be tilted toward the rear at the top. This variation from vertical is the *caster* angle. Thus, if the imaginary line is extended to ground level, it will intersect the ground at a point ahead of the center of the tire contact patch, which gives the steering a "self-centering" effect. A caster angle gauging function is included with most all camber gauges.

In practice, the "straight-ahead" position of the wheels is established, then they are turned (usually) 20 degrees to the left or right, and the caster gauge leveled. Turning the wheels all the way past zero to 20 degrees the opposite way yields (after the gauge is again leveled) a reading on a separate bubble vial that is calibrated directly in degrees of caster angle. The caster gauge reads the change in camber that results from steering the wheels. (Imagine an absurdly large caster angle, say 45 degrees. If the front wheels could then be steered through 90 degrees, each would exhibit 45 degrees of camber.) Note that some passenger cars have used *negative* caster, and that some "left-turn-only" race cars have different amounts of caster on each side.

While caster/camber gauges usually have surfaces on the case that are arranged at plus and minus 20 degrees to straight ahead, to aid "eyeballing" caster, some way to precisely measure the steer angle of the wheels is preferable. A tool to permit such measurement is the "turn plate"—simply a ball bearing-equipped platform (obviously, a pair is required) that each front wheel rests on, and provided with protractor-like markings around its edge, at one degree intervals. With the wheels arranged dead ahead, the turn plate is zeroed by a movable pointer. Steer angles can now be read out with precision.

Digital instruments have penetrated here, too. While their cost and complication are probably not justifiable for caster measurements, as described above, the extremely high accuracy of digital turn plates allows them to be used to establish another variable—the "Ackerman" effect. To understand this, we have to go back a long way in history, to the earliest horse-drawn wagons. On these, as on a child's coaster wagon, steering is accomplished by

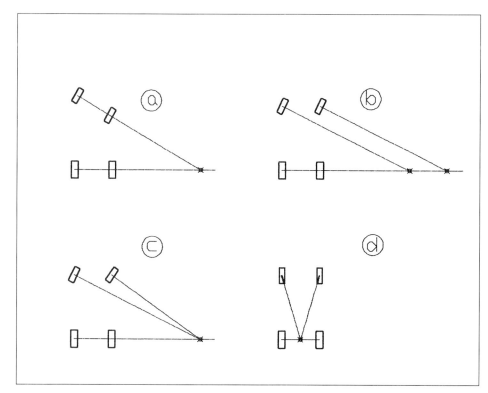

When the entire front axle steers, as on a wagon (a), each wheel rolls around a single turn center. If front wheels steer individually, but each steers through the same angle (b), then each front wheel rolls around a different point; there is no single center of the turn and a lot of tire scrub will occur. If the inner wheel is turned through a larger angle than the outer one (c), then a single turn center can be restored. Theoretically, to achieve that, the steering arms have to be inclined so their lines would intersect at a point in the middle of the rear axle (d). This is Ackerman steering.

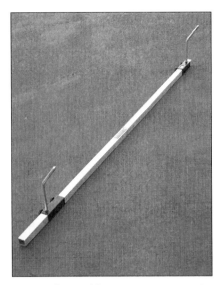

It is usually possible to measure across the front of a pair of front tires at axle height using a tape measure, but at the rear the car usually gets in the way. A length of square tubing with a couple of long, sliding pointers can solve the problem. You can make your own, or buy a production item. *Longacre Automotive Racing Products*

skewing the entire front axle relative to the frame. Obviously, a line drawn through a steered front axle will intersect a line drawn through the fixed rear axle at some distance from the vehicle centerline. Now, theoretically, this point of intersection is the center around which the whole vehicle will steer.

The appearance of individual wheel steering introduced a new problem: If the steering arms extend straight forward (or straight back), each wheel will steer through the same angle, so now there will be *three* axes—one through the fixed rear axle, plus one for each of the two front wheels, leading to considerable

wheel scrub. Mr. Ackerman realized this, and so arranged for the steering arms on his carriage to be inclined so that a line drawn from the kingpin axis through the outer steering swivel on each side would intersect exactly at the center of the rear axle. This, theoretically, eliminated steering scrub when cornering, at least at one specific steer angle.

Although inflatable rubber tires behave very differently from steel-shod wagon wheels, this Ackerman effect remains important. Now, perfect Ackerman steering is *not* desirable on race cars, but to optimize the setup it is sometimes important to directly measure the

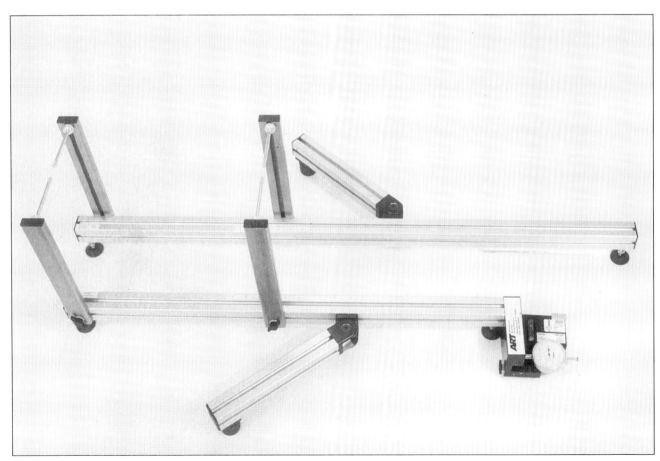

The very latest in alignment equipment is laser equipped. This laser toe gauge achieves unprecedented accuracy; some pro teams wouldn't leave home without one. *Advanced Racing Technologies, Inc.*

difference in steer angle between the two front wheels at various positions. For this, a turn plate of very high precision is needed, hence the digital turn plate. One commercial unit resolves to 0.1 degrees, 10 times finer than passive, "protractor"-type plates.

Also of concern is toe-in/toe-out. This is the extent to which the front wheels (and the rears, in the case of independent rear suspension) are steered toward or away from each other when nominally pointing straight ahead. This is purely a linear measurement problem, usually performed by measuring the distance between the centerlines of the tires at axle height, both ahead and behind the axle. The difference between these measurements is the toe-in (or out).

Two problems attend measuring toe-in. First is establishing the centerline of each tire. In fact, it need not be the exact centerline, but the reference points have to lie in a plane at right angles to the spindle axis. The easy way to do this is to jack up the front end, spin each wheel by hand, and, using a scriber of some sort, scratch a line around each front tire. Specialized, spring-loaded scribing tools are available; a firmly held screwdriver rocking on an oil can works about as well. A rub with chalk before scribing will improve the legibility of the line.

The second problem is measuring the spacing between these lines at both the front and rear of the tires. The front is usually no bother at all, and can be established to perhaps 1/32-inch accuracy with a steel tape. Often, though, the measurement of this distance at the back edges of the tire is hampered because of machinery in the way. A

Bump-steer is the tendency of front wheels to steer left or right as the suspension moves through its travel. This jig is designed to help measure bump steer. Most of the rig simply sits on the floor; the steering tendency of a plate secured to the hub is measured by a pair of dial indicators as it slides up and down through wheel movement. *Longacre Automotive Racing Products*

length of, say, 3/4-inch steel tube with two long pointers sticking out at right angles—one fixed and one adjustable—allows sneaking up on the problem from below.

For a time there were optical gauges that permitted measuring of toe-in/toe-out with considerably higher accuracy than can be achieved with a steel tape, but these now seem to have disappeared. The latest technology to be applied to toe measurements involves the use of lasers. This is a very recent development that is just now appearing in the highest ranks of racing. Since both the technology and the market (and, for that matter, regulations regarding the safety of lasers) are in flux, we will withhold comment for a later edition of this book.

Finally, there is the measurement of "bump-steer." To explain, the geometric "fight" between steering linkages and suspension linkages means that when a steerable wheel moves upward over bumps (and downward in

rebound) it almost always also steers slightly to one side or the other. To eliminate this, or at least minimize it, usually by changing the vertical position of the inboard steering ball-joints, it is necessary to measure the phenomenon. This is usually achieved by blocking the car up so the suspension can droop to full rebound, removing the spring and damper, then manually cycling the wheel through its range of suspension travel while measuring its steering tendency with a jig.

The jig comprises a plate bolted to the wheel mounting flange, plus a hinged fixture, one-half of which rests on the ground, while the other half supports a pair of dial indicators, one each at the front and rear edges of the plate. For street, road race, and drag cars, a measurement with the wheels pointed straight ahead is usual; oval track cars usually arrange for zero bump steer with a couple of degrees of left turn steering dialed in.

CONVERSION FACTORS FOR PRESSURE

1 inch water	= 249.09 Pa
1 inch water	= 0.0025 atmospheres
1 inch water	= 0.0361 lbf/sq inch
1 inch Hg	= 3.3864 kPa
1 inch Hg	= 0.0333 atmospheres
1 inch Hg	= 0.489 lbf/sq inch
1 mm Hg	= 133.32 Pa
1 mm Hg	= 0.0013 atmospheres
1 mm Hg	= 0.019 lbf/sq inch
1 std. atmosphere	= 101.24 kPa
1 std. atmosphere	= 29.92 inch Hg
1 std. atmosphere	= 14.694 lbf/sq inch
1 Pa	= 0.10197 mm H2O
1 kPa	= 4.0146 inch H2O
1 kPa	= 0.2953 inch Hg
1 kPa	= 7.5006 mm Hg
1 kPa	= 10 millibar (mb)
1 kPa	= 0.14504 lbf/sq inch
100 kPa	= 0.9869 atmos.
1000 kPa	= 0.1097 kgf/sq mm
1 bar	= 100 kPa
1 lbf/sq inch	= 6.8948 kPa
1 lbf/sq inch	= 2.04 inch Hg
1 kgf/sq mm	= 9806.65 kPa

INDEX

Accuracy, definition of, 11, 12
Air density meters, 100, 101
Alignment gauges and tools, 118–123
Ammeter, see Multimeters
Analog versus digital measurements, 15, 16
Angle finder, see Inclinometers
Angle gauges, 71, 73
Angular measurements, 62, 63
Balances, see Mechanical weight scales
Beam balances, 79
Bevel protractors, 66–68
Bore micrometers, 57, 58
Bourdon tube, 94, 95
Brown, J.R., 28
Burette, 116–118
Caster/camber gauges, 117–122
Center heads, 20
Combination squares, 19, 20
Cylinder leakage testers, see Leak-down testers
Depth gauges, 59–61
Dial bore gauges, 56–59
Dial calipers, 21–23
Dial depth gauges, 60
Dial indicators, 36–43
    Use of, 41–43
Dial test indicators, 43–45
Drill gauges, 24, 26, 27
Electronic weigh scales, 81–83
Ellstrom, Hjalmar, 13
Fixed gauges, 26, 27, 71, 73, 74
Force gauges, 83–86
Gascoigne, 28
Gauge blocks, 44, 46, 71
Graduated beaker, 116
Graduated cylinders, 117
Height gauges, 26, 27
Hoke, Major William, 13
Inclinometers, 65–67
Infrared (IR) pyrometer, 111, 113
Inside calipers, 47, 48
Inside micrometers, 52–57

Interchangeable parts, 10
International System of Weights and Measures, see Metric System
Johansson, C.E., 13
Laser toe gauge, 122, 123
Leak-down testers, 97–99
Leland, Henry, 10
Levels, 64–67
Liquid-in-glass thermometers, 105, 106
Machinist's rules, 17–20
Machinist's squares, 64
Manometers, 92–94
Mechanical weight scales, 78, 79, 81
Metric conversion factors, 16
Metric system, 16
Micrometer calipers, 28–38
Micrometer depth gauges, 61
Micrometers,
    Checking for accuracy, 36
    Digital, 31
    Reading of, 31, 32
    Use of, 34–38
Multimeters, 102–105
    Use of, 105
Optical flat, 32
Optical parallel, 32
Outside calipers, 20–22
Palmer, 28
Parallels, 63, 64
Performance, increasing, 10
Plastigage, 54
Plug thread gauges, 74, 75
Precision, definition of, 11, 12
Pressure gauges, 92–96
Pressure, units of, 95
Protractor heads, 19
Pyrometers, 107, 108
Radius gauges, 73, 75
Reference standards, 12–14
Road spring rate checkers, 83–86
Rule holders, see Rule stands

Rule stands, 19
Screw pitch gauges (thread gauges), 73
Screw threads, measuring, 73–77
Sharpe, Lucian, 28
Significant digits, 13
Sine bar, 71
Slide calipers, 20, 22–24, 26, 48, 49
   Digital, 22, 23
   Use of, 24, 26
Small hole gauges, 51, 52
Speed of light, use for measuring, 14
Spring scales, 81
Stagger tapes, 18
Starrett, Laroy, 28
Straightedges, 63
Stroboscopes, 113, 114
Surface plates, 25
Systéme International (SI), see Metric system
Tachometers, 112–114
Tape measures, 17, 18
Taper gauges, 49
Telescoping gauges, 49–52
Temperature calibration points, 108

Temperature, 105–113
Thermal expansion, 18
Thermocouples, 107, 108–111
Thermometers, dial, 106, 107
Thickness (feeler) gauges, 52, 53
Thread gauging micrometers, 77
Timing lights, 114–116
Timing wheels/degree wheels, 68–70
Tire pressure gauges, digital, 96, 97
Toe in/toe out, measuring, 123
Torque wrenches, 86–92
   Bending beam type, 87–89
   Click type, 89, 90
   Dial type, 89
   Use of, 91, 92
Trigonometry, 72
Vernier calipers, 22–24, 26, 28
Vernier depth gauges, 59, 60
Vernier micrometers, 31–34
   Reading of, 34
Vernier protractors, 67, 68
Vernier scale, 21, 22
Volt/ohmeter (VOM) see Multimeters
Volume, measuring, 116–118
Wire gauges, 24, 26, 27